# I Wandered Lonely as a Cloud

*I wandered lonely as a cloud*
*That floats on high o'er vales and hills,*
*When all at once I saw a crowd,*
*A host, of golden daffodils;*
*Beside the lake, beneath the trees,*
*Fluttering and dancing in the breeze.*

*Continuous as the stars that shine*
*And twinkle on the milky way,*
*They stretched in never-ending line*
*Along the margin of a bay:*
*Ten thousand saw I at a glance,*
*Tossing their heads in sprightly dance.*

*The waves beside them danced; but they*
*Out-did the sparkling waves in glee:*
*A poet could not but be gay,*
*In such a jocund company:*
*I gazed – and gazed – but little thought*
*What wealth the show to me had brought:*

*For oft, when on my couch I lie*
*In vacant or in pensive mood,*
*They flash upon that inward eye*
*Which is the bliss of solitude;*
*And then my heart with pleasure fills,*
*And dances with the daffodils.*

William Wordsworth (1815)

ISIS

# Prism of Solitude

## Introverts' Heaven

© 2021 ISIS
Cover: ISIS
Illustration: ISIS, Sabine Sparakowski
Editing: ISIS & OSIRIS
Publishing and Print: tredition GmbH, Halenreie 40-44, 22359 Hamburg

ISBN
978-3-347-04419-7 (Paperback)
978-3-347-04420-3 (Hardcover)
978-3-347-04421-0 (e-Book)

Bibliographic information of the Deutsche Nationalbibliothek: The Deutsche Nationalbibliothek lists this publication in the Deutsche Nationalbibliografie. Detailed data are available via internet: see website http://dnb.d-nb.de.

# Contents

# Contents

# Dedication

This book is mainly dedicated to my *mother* and my *daughter*. Very often, I think of us as a *'Spiritual Trinity of Introverts'*. We shine like candles that no storm can dim. Our souls seem to be intertwined in mystical patterns of different destinies.

Of course, I dedicate this book to my *friends*. Astonishingly almost all of them are introverts. That's why we get along so well. Our friendships are a beautiful tapestry of respect and tolerance. With each other, we can be who we are. Thank you for being in my life and filling it with so much joy.

The book is also dedicated to all other *readers*, whom I want to encourage in taking control of their own lives.

# Introduction

When I started writing the first chapter of this book, it happened under the most unusual circumstances. It was on the 22nd of March in 2020. The whole world was in a deuce of a stir and on the verge of collapsing. If 3 months ago, I had been told that we are in for a world-wide flu pandemic, I would not have believed it.

The last time a pandemic of this enormity happened, was the *Spanish flu*, also known as the *1918 flu pandemic*. It lasted to December 1920. Nobody knew where the Spanish flu had originally started. But we know that in December 2019, the coronavirus disease, COVID-19, was allegedly first detected in China. In no time, the infection had spread to a steadily increasing number of countries around the world. Of course, everyone here hoped that Europe would escape the disaster that followed. How little we knew…

At first, the reported symptoms like dry cough, fever and tiredness did not appear as that serious. In mild cases, people just got a sore throat or a runny nose. Then, there were more severe effects as breathing difficulties and organ failure. All too soon, the fatalities soared. Now, that got nearly everyone's attention.

Eventually, the inevitable happened. On the 11th of March 2020, the World Health Organisation (WHO) declared the outbreak a pandemic. From that moment on, the German government started to act in ways we never experienced before. Soon, my company followed suit with new and more alarming bulletins every day. First, we were not allowed to travel between the locations of our company anymore. Then, restrictions were imposed regarding journeys to other countries and even within Germany. Afterwards, most of the employees had to work in their home offices, and the German government was short of declaring a curfew. The latter happened 9 months later.

At this point, I discovered once more the advantages of being an introverted person. It can be a real blessing in disguise. Unlike most of my colleagues, who disliked the very thought of being confined to their homes, I thrived on it. Finally, I could live a life I always had been dreaming of, if only for a while. Alone in my quiet home which is my *castle*, I worked undisturbed and in complete solitude. Every day, I got up in my own time, and my meals were freshly cooked.

The best of it, I was not forced to listen to that shallow gossip and small talk in the office anymore. What an ironic blessing, coming out of humankind's latest curse! Maybe, I should have felt guilty about not panicking like lots of people, but I did not. There are always two sides of a coin, just like there are darkness and light. I have chosen the latter. People who panic, cannot think clearly, - a state I abhor in myself.

It sounds cruel, but there is no better time than a pandemic to start writing a book. There are neither disturbances nor excuses, so I decided to make the best of it. A lot of inspiration I took from *Jenn Granneman's* website https://introvertdear.com. How she approached the sensitive topic of introversion, I liked very much, especially the non-scientific parts. When I sat down to structure this book, I decided to reflect on selected topics about introversion. *Jenn* mentioned that there are no two introverts who are alike. It was fun to prove her point in exploring the inner world of my family and other people based on the described signs of introversion.

Most of the illustrations in my book are cut-outs I made about forty years ago, which I will come back to in another chapter. There is also one Zentangle painting by my friend S., who loves to spend her evenings drawing, which she is very creative at.

# Who we are

Who we are poses a question to which there are many answers. They also change with the years, depending on our states of spiritual growth. There are numerous different influencing factors, for example, intentional personality changes that take years to flower. Nevertheless, I think that what our spirits bring to this world is even more crucial. Some characteristics are difficult or impossible to change, such as temperament or introversion. The best thing we can do is to recognise who we really are and accept ourselves as unique, magnificent beings. Unfortunately, this is often denied to us by our upbringing at home or in school. Far too soon, we are snatched away from the world of magic and wonder, only to be moulded into service-ready recruits for the economy. It still seems to be the aim of society to subdue a person's creative thinking and work, to nip any revolutionary movement in the bud.

As to be expected, introverts are "*sensitive to different things. Psychologist Jonathan Cheek, along with graduate students Jennifer Grimes and*

*Courtney Brown, wanted to explore these differences. They hypothesized that there are different types of introverts, or in other words, different ways in which a person's introversion can be expressed."* They divided introverts into 4 categories: the *"social"*, the *"thinking"*, the *"anxious"*, and the *"restrained"*. It made me think about my own family, and I discovered clear distinctions between our introverted natures.

(Jenn Granneman. March 10, 2015. Introvert, Dear. Retrieved from https://introvertdear.com/news/science-says-there-are-4-kinds-of-introverts)

Now and again, I write about my mother as if she were still alive, for in my heart, she is and always will be. Since our spirits and souls are immortal, the bond between us is as strong as it was before she passed away.

## Reflection on 'social' Introverts

As it turns out, all the three of us are *'social'* introverts indeed. We do not like hanging out with more than two people at one time. As a matter of fact, we prefer not to meet with anyone too often at all. We love being alone and being left alone, except by our loved ones. In a world dominated by extroverts, this can be difficult and sometimes impossible. Of course, it also depends on how strongly one can make a stand.

## My Mother

My mother was born in 1925, and her youth was determined by the Second World War. The most gentle, loving soul, she was as strong as she was quiet. In times of solitude, I take out our black and white family pictures. There, I see a beautiful, slender woman who does not like to be in the limelight. My mother must have been about 17 years old then. Smiling, she stands shyly beside a grazing horse in the meadow of her aunt's property. It was summer, and her life seemed to spread before her as lavishly as the flowers around her. I bet she liked to dance across that meadow when nobody saw her. Her innocence and purity come across in such a touching way. I wish I had known her in those days. Her brother R. and her sister J. were also introverts. The siblings loved each other very much.

Somehow, my mother struggled through the years of war, which must have been hard. Afterwards, she began an education as a teacher, where she met my father. Later, my parents showed me pictures with their first school classes. Nowadays, it is unthinkable that one person teaches forty pupils of different ages at once and in one classroom. Nonetheless, they managed quite well. When I discovered that my mother was an introvert, I wondered how she could stand in front of a class, much less working as a director of her school years later. Now I know why. She was well-endowed with talents no one knew about. The pupils respected and adored her at the same time.

My mother had an incredible aura. She emanated this rare kind of quiet, yet unyielding strength, paired with love for everyone, especially the prodigal sons. Often in the afternoons, she used her spare time to teach them extra lessons, but without a wagging finger or moral sermons. Instead, she encouraged the kids to explore their own limits and not to give up.

My mother's *social* introversion obviously did not show in her profession as a teacher. Maybe, we can't survive in our jobs without a certain kind of armour. In her private life, though, she was different. In a way, her home was just another kind of battlefield. Mind you, she was a mother of four daughters. Both of my parents worked fulltime. These days, mothers can stay at home for years until their children start school. Back then in East-Germany, the women did not have this privilege. Six weeks after giving birth, they were forced back to fulltime work. As much as I tried, I could never imagine where she took the strength from to bear this heavy burden.

It is ironic and sad that my mother's social introversion did not have the chance to become a disadvantage at all, because she did not have the time to socialise at all. As long as we children lived at home, she simply had not one minute for herself.

During the week in the morning, she got up at 5.30 and made breakfast for everyone. After making the beds, she went to school before we left the house. Having returned in the afternoon, there were the usual chores to do: shopping, cleaning, and cooking. Late in the evenings, from spring to autumn, my father used to come back from our distant garden with plenty of fruits and vegetables. Proudly, he put them on the kitchen table, not being aware of my mother's tired, weary looking eyes. It reminds me of a certain caveman behaviour, what with the man throwing the game on the floor, expecting the cavewoman to see to it immediately. It has not changed that much, or has it?

Now, my mother's third shift began, because everything had to be cleaned, chopped, and cooked or canned. When she was finished with all that, there were still the tasks of doing the preparations for the next day's lessons, and she did them very thoroughly. It was about one in the morning, sometimes later, when she went to bed, totally exhausted. I am ashamed to admit that I never realised this until I was an adult myself. Thinking back to my adolescence, I regret not having been more helpful and understanding, instead of mouthing off to her. Oh well!

My mother's social life mostly happened within her family boundaries. Of course, there were a few occasions such as birthday parties. Again, she was the one who did all the work to make them successful. When she finally had the chance to sit down, she felt comfortable amongst her guests, for they were family and very close friends. However, the peaceful moments didn't last. At some point, my father started speaking and did not stop until the party ended. He saw himself as an entertainer. It might have been funny if he hadn't always stolen my mother's show or told the same stories for the hundredth time. Whatever had happened, *he* was the only hero. Of course, it was never my mother, although in reality it was just the other way around.

When I was older, I attended the family birthday parties too. There, I observed that as soon as my mother started speaking, my father cut her off. Don't get me wrong, in his way, he loved her deeply, but he obviously could not help himself, being a distinct extrovert. My father worked hard, but my mother carried much more weight than he did. He picked the tasks that suited him most: his work, his sport, and his garden. My mother could do nothing of this sort. It was the way many marriages worked back then.

Then, there were the weekends. After lunch, when the dishes were done, finally my mother's time had come. First, she sat down in her rocking chair to read the paper. Afterwards, she indulged in reading one of her favourite books until she fell asleep and enjoyed a most welcome siesta. The books were either crime novels or fantasy stories. Those were the hours she loved the most: being alone and being left alone to do what she liked.

Although we lived in a house with other families, I never saw my mother making small-talk with them. On the one hand, she did not have the time, and on the other hand, she simply was not interested in any kind of social contact with others. Once, I asked her if she did not miss having a close friend. Smiling sadly, she told me that there was one in her childhood days, but no, she does not want other friends anymore.

## My Daughter

Now that I write about my mother's situation, it is somewhat terrifying how similar my daughter is in this regard too. She was a lovely and cheerful child. Most of the years, I raised her alone. In East-Germany, there was no such thing as unemployment. Everyone had the duty to work fulltime; men and women alike. We never questioned it. For us, it was normal.

During the week at about 6 in the morning, I left my daughter at the nearby nursery. She hated being abandoned by me every day anew, always crying when I went away. It was heart-breaking and I felt like a poor mother. Unlike other children in the nursery, my daughter never took a nap after lunch. According to the nurses, one of them had to watch her closely. Otherwise, my mentally stressed daughter tended to tear out strands of her beautiful dark hair. In hindsight, I suspect she did not feel comfortable away from me. When I picked her up in the afternoon at about 5.30, it had been a long day for her. She seemed to be content, but was quite exhausted too. One could tell that being with strangers had taken its toll.

Occasionally, my daughter liked to play with children in the neighbourhood. She preferred to socialize with one at a time, though. At the weekends, she loved to go with me down to the river. Surrounded by water and trees, she could roam free and undisturbed. Nature provided us with everything. With her, I felt like a kid again.

Also, she spent hours and days at home in her room. In solitude, she played happily with her dolls or patiently built little cities and zoos on the carpet. I still remember her daily question: *"Mama, will you play with me?"* With the tight schedule, it was difficult, but I tried to spend as much time as possible with my *Little Rosebud.* As soon as she could, she liked to read books. During the years, we moved house frequently about the country. Wherever we settled, my daughter had a few good friends she liked to spend time with. She was living a much less secluded life back then. In her adolescence, my daughter did not attend many parties. She tried because it seemed the normal thing to do. But soon she discovered that she did not like deafening noise, crowds of people and the quantities of alcohol one was supposed to drink. Then, there came a time when she did not want to leave the house at all. Most of the time, she stayed in her room, reading, dancing, watching TV, and day-dreaming. My daughter was part of a girl's group who shared the dislike of parties. They attended the same school class and sometimes met in their free time in twos and threes. So, she had her fair share of socializing in a way that suited her the most.

My daughter's life as an adult started a far cry from my mother's or mine. She did not have any children. From an early age on, she lived with her boyfriend. Since then, she con-centrated mainly on their relationship. With a fulltime job and a household to maintain, this is enough on one's plate. Living a very private life, she let her socializing dwindle even fur-ther. Just like me, she is more than satisfied to stay home in her happy place of solitude. For-tunately, with the right partner, to enjoy soli-tude doesn't necessarily imply to be alone.

## Myself

Where does that leave me as the third part of our *'Spiritual Trinity of Introverts'*? Taking a walk down memory lane, I realised that I have roamed many fascinating pathways. More than half a century ago, I was born as the third child of my parents. I take that as a good sign. The third child in the Fairy tales was always the pick of the bunch, the hero and the saviour. I liked that very much. Besides, three is a magical number!

Well, having two older sisters was no means a bed of roses. At least not in my case! For a start, they did not like each other. This showed in the occasional catfights, where hair has been ripped out in sibling rivalries. Plus, my second sister was jealous of me. It has not changed to this day and must be something she has been born with. My parents told us that as a baby, she regularly demanded a second helping of food. My sister just would not shut up until she got it or was hoarse from screeching.

I never felt comfortable around my older siblings. Having been the favourite of my father, as I have been told, did not improve the matter. I agree with *Rudolf Steiner* going as far as to say that my spirit might have chosen my parents, but there is no way it has singled out my older sisters. At least the regular fights with them prepared me well for the battles in the business world yet to come. Eventually, everything turned for the better when my younger sister came to see the light of day. Close in age, we used to play with each other peacefully. She was a delightful, easy-going and amiable child, and to this day we get along well together.

Although my parents never said so, I was a difficult child. I have been blessed with a divinely explosive mixture of a choleric and sanguine temperament. True, my melancholic side flared briefly during adolescence but calmed down when I became a mother. As for my phlegmatic part, I swear that it is practically non-existent.

Of the first two mentioned temperaments, I got the best. My choleric nature provides me with an abundance of energy and willpower, coming from my spirit's deep well. It allows me to tap into unfailing sources of power that overrides my physical strength manifold. To the sanguine temper, I owe my figure, inner joy, and flexibility. It also supplies me with a good memory, keen perception, and an enquiring mind.

How did my *social* introversion show in my childhood days? It was a mix back then. Naturally, within our home, I was forced to play by the rules of the family. This meant to be present at the table during meals and to do the chores together with my sisters. The latter didn't always end well, because I was a born fighter and put up with nothing. In my early childhood photographs, you can see a thoughtful, fearless hoyden who was ready to accept any challenge. It is visible evidence that I had no desire to conform to anyone's rules except my own.

In kindergarten, I was forced to adjust to the rules of the group in a not so different way. Already, I had my own ideas on how to cope with the situation. Not that keen on playing with other children, I wanted to be left alone. However, there was a huge magnet, so to speak, which pulled me back every time. You might not believe it, but it was the dolls' prams. There were three of them, and only the fastest children were lucky enough to get to play with them. Sadly, my innermost wish to have one at home has never been satisfied.

A day in kindergarten started with breakfast at those tiny tables, reminding me of Snow White and the Seven Dwarfs. A wooden chandelier with coloured figures from Fairy tales hung from the ceiling. They fascinated me every day anew because my whole world consisted of Fairy tales. They were my centre and my sanity all the time.

After breakfast, our kindergarten teacher gave the signal for the raid on the toys. Instantly, my conditioned reflexes kicked in. To the other children's disappointment, I won the race nearly every day. To be honest, it was not fair. From the age of 4, I had started training in the swimming pool with my father. This gave me the chance to hone my physical skills three times a week.

Anyway, as soon as I got hold of my favourite toy, I began playing with the dolls, alone. I suppose that's where my intensive wish to become a mother arose from. Happily submerged in a world of bliss and inner solitude, I was rarely aware of other children around me. Little did I know how demanding it is to be a mother!

Vividly, I remember a girl who became a very close friend when I was a child. From the beginning, there was a strong bond between us. Our families habitually spent their summer holidays together in a bungalow. Unfortunately, her family lived quite a distance away from us. Later, it did not matter that there was no communication for years. Some friendships last forever, even without words.

I did not have many close friends during the first school years, though. One reason might have been the fact that I changed schools three times. When homework was done and I was not busy with sports, I liked to hang out with kids from the neighbourhood. I would not call it friendship that bound us together. Only now do I realize that all of them were introverts too. The communication between us I remember as awkward. One day, the bunch of us went to the nearby woods. You may not believe it, but it was a magical forest. Legend has it that beyond the small doors in the hillside, the witches dwelt. Oh, what a thrilling feeling that was! We also loved to build huge nests in the hedges around the house, pretending to be squirrels gathering supplies for the winter. There was a special smell to the dried grass we used for the padding. I will never forget it, and it is firmly linked to the memory of happy summer days.

When the weather was not pleasant enough to go out, I hunkered down in the room I shared with my youngest sister. There, a stack of books was patiently waiting for me. My mother used to lovingly call me her *bookworm*. When I got caught up in my reading, I totally forgot about time and the world around me.

The public library was a 30 minutes' walk away, but I did not mind carrying the books. They were my treasures, and going to the library was always a special treat for me. It was located in the mystical castle on the outskirts of the city. A sturdy bridge traversed the moat, where once fallow deer had been herded. After crossing the viaduct, I turned left to open one of the oldest and creakiest doors I ever came across. The grey stones of a long stairway were impossibly worn-away. The typical musty smell of the old castle was strangely familiar. Reverently, I tiptoed upstairs, holding my breath. Then, something incredible happened that never fails to enchant me anew. Heavenly music drifted by, stopping me in my tracks. Aside from the library, this part of the castle also hosted the music school.

Leisurely, I walked through the magnificent rooms, passing along high bookshelves, my mind slowly merging with the music and the stories in the books. Every time, my heart started aching because I so longed to play an instrument. More than once, I had asked my parents about that. Unfortunately, with four children, they could not afford the costs of music lessons. I was old enough to understand that every child in our family should have the same opportunities. So it was just not in the cards for us. That was when I took an oath. *"One day, when my children are grown-up, I will learn to play the piano or the violin."* Well, I kept my promise. I did learn to play the piano and later discovered my love for the Celtic Harp, which I play until today.

From the age of 11, I was trained as a professional swimmer for many years. Together with my youngest sister, I lived abroad in a residential school. As one can imagine, there was no time for socializing whatsoever. Two times a day, we attended lessons at school. The rest of the time, we spent swimming or doing other kinds of sport. This went on from Monday to Saturday. Our trainers ran a tight ship, which required a lot of discipline on our side. The teachers were very understanding and treated us accordingly with patience when we were tired from training. Looking back, I admit that I did not miss the socializing part at all.

During the last four school years, I befriended one girl especially. We are still in contact. Alas, aside from the swimming practice, we never spent any quality time with each other. Her family was a busy lot, and she already had a boyfriend. But I was quite content to live a solitary life. Throughout my studies and afterwards while raising my daughter, I have not had time or interest in actively fostering friendships. For a while, friendships from my childhood were on hold. We all raised our children and were busy with family matters. Loosely, we stayed in contact via phone, email, or letters and reconnected years later as if no time had passed at all.

## Friends Forever

*We were always drawn*
*To the same kind of man*
*We never intervened*
*Respecting each other*

*They used to call us Twins*
*Sometimes I wondered why*
*Kept apart by distance*
*For years, we didn't meet*
*Yet, here we are: as close*
*As true friends can be*

*How could we have known*
*We'd never lose that bond?*
*So, as time goes on, we will*
*Be in our hearts, forever*

ISIS (2017)

This is what real friendship is about: it cannot be broken. We did not lose sight of each other, but adjusted to the changes in our lives. My balance recalibrated considerably when my daughter left home to live with her boyfriend. Can you imagine that until then, I was not aware that my daughter and I are introverted?

One should think that now could have been the time to socialize. It was strange, though. When my daughter had left, I kept myself hanging in a very odd state for at least three months. I was not sure what to make of it. It felt as if someone had removed my right arm or my heart. I had this queer picture of myself as a startled turtle that had existed for too long in a frozen state. Thus, it was now afraid to push its head out from under its carapace. That was the same feeling I had when I stopped pushing my daughter's buggy. At the age of 15 months, she had insistently declared not to use it anymore. Obviously, I was afraid to use my newly won freedom properly. I was totally out of practise to have time for myself.

Fortunately, this state did not last forever. At some point, my inner joy must have returned. Slowly, all these frozen parts of me that had been repressed over the last 20 years came to life again. Mainly via the internet, I began to build new friendships with other introverted people. Most of the time, we keep to ourselves. Now and again, I meet with them. On such one-to-one contacts, we enjoy each other's company thoroughly. After laughing, joking, and having good talks, we return to our self-chosen solitude. Astonishingly, afterwards we don't feel drained at all.

Now and again, I like to go on vacation in places where there are preferably no people around. The only ongoing activities are planned by me. I rarely stay in hotels, but prefer to rent a cottage, where I have my freedom and quietude. Whenever I travelled with groups, I regretted it afterwards, at least partly. Of course, we had plenty of fun together, but the older I become, the harder it gets to adjust to a group's dynamic.

## Reflection on 'thinking' Introverts

According to *Jonathan Cheek, "a "thinking" introvert is someone who is introspective, thoughtful, and self-reflective. This person daydreams and enjoys losing themselves in their inner fantasy world."*

(Jenn Granneman. March 10, 2015. Introvert, Dear. Retrieved from https://introvertdear.com/news/science-says-there-are-4-kinds-of-introverts)

Well, now we are talking! The world to make sense logically is a necessity for us introverts. How the world works is reflected by an internal network, which is steadily being improved through life experience. Extroverted people might find this illogical, though. Any kind of knowledge, the mind automatically weaves into a tapestry of interrelated information. Obviously, this aptitude enables us to find commonalities in seemingly unrelated things. It definitely makes me great at troubleshooting. Deep down, I want to know how everything works together, and I don't rest until we know all the related components. That explains why I was always good at support matters.

It is also said that introverted thinking involves a desire for truth. I second that, but it is not always easy to tell what the truth is. If two people confirm sight of a red chair and one person is colour-blind, what is the truth then? Is the chair red or not? *Johann Wolfgang von Goethe* had an interesting theory about that.

Although I have wondered why it takes me a while to see the light at times, there is nothing wrong with my intelligence. I guess it is because I want to get to the bottom of things, and I am not satisfied with simple explanations. Neither am I inclined to talk about matters unless I fully understand them.

I don't know about my mother, but my daughter and I are good at self-reflection. It took us a while to get there, though. In 2000, I had a serious breakdown due to many years of living in the fast lane. That forced me to work out a strategy not just to survive, but to add action to the self-reflection. It was essential to overcome and change habitual traits. It is not enough to reflect on things and to realize what's to be done. Everything is in vain if we do not act on our insights. For me, this is the hardest part.

My daughter and I indeed have the tendency to daydream and yes, we enjoy losing ourselves in the inner fantasy world. Not that any of us had or has much time for daydreaming, but we take what we get. It is something we like and indulge in whenever we get the chance. Usually, we are good at hiding the fact that we are doing it. Daydreaming is not just a means to escape the downsides of the extroverts' world, but an essential strategy to recharge the batteries.

The beauty of dwelling in the inner fantasy world lies in the fact that nobody can take this away from us. It is not just one world, but we are talking about endless galaxies of parallel existing realities here. This is the very stage, where we test our skills for the hero's journey in realms where we cannot fail, but triumph and rejoice.

Once, my daughter told me about her kind of daydreaming when reading a book with a rather inconvenient outcome. If there is no happy end and the stupid hero dies instead of living happily ever after with his beloved, she rewrites the finish in her head. She just cannot bear it when the lovers are doomed, neither can I. I've even got the tendency to never read another one of this particular author's books again. If we want stories that make us unhappy, we just look around in the neighbourhood. We read books to be uplifted, inspired and to be encouraged instead of mentally dragged down.

Another way to express the inner fantasy within a protected setting is dancing at home when no one is looking. Alone, one feels free and connected with the spirit and the music, - gliding and swaying gracefully in harmony with the rhythm. This is pure happiness and joy.

As *thinking* introverts we are capable of drawing courage, power, and wisdom from an inexhaustible well of possibilities. Extroverted people might see this just as a mere escape from reality and an excuse for coping, but it is not.

There is another barely describable pleasure we experience in our family, at least when it comes to my mother and me. We do not just love to read, but also to write poems and prose. Unfortunately, my mother neither had the time nor chance to develop her writing skills any further. I learned only about her talent when I found a few written pieces after she had died. That's a great pity! She could have taught me so many things.

At the age of 8, I wrote my first poem. It was about one of the old, glorious paintings *'The Singing Boys'* by *Frans Hals*, and of course, the verses rhymed. I am a sucker for rhyme, no matter that some of the modern poets scorn it. Besides, I assume that their critique might partly derive from a lack of ability to rhyme. Do you know how difficult it is to learn a poem by heart when the words don't rhyme? Tell me about it!

Already as a child, I enjoyed making up stories in my mind. The real writing came later. But I wrote long letters to my friends who loved to read them. They said: *"You write just as you speak."* When the mood strikes me, I can be quite the comedienne and like to express myself in untypical ways. Also, I am known for using old and almost forgotten words that make others laugh.

When it comes to fulfilling wishes or desires, working with fantasy and daydreaming can be very helpful indeed. When first I started reading about the right technique for making a proper wish, I did not take the matter seriously. As it happened, the experience put me right. For a wish to be fulfilled, it must be formed in the present tense. So, if one is good at fantasizing, then to wish successfully should be a walk in the park.

Nowadays, my daughter and I also nurture our fantasies in reading entertaining fantasy novels. Then, we can dive into worlds where everything is possible, and nothing seems strange to us. Like joyful Fairies, we dance happily on top of mysterious waves of words, knowing we cannot drown or be destroyed. As the stories of our childhood, fantasy books take us into realms of magic and love. Even these days, we still like to read Fairy tales or watch similar films.

One of the best traits of being an introvert is to be introspective, that is, to analyse oneself.

It takes a great deal of courage, endurance and solitude to do it thoroughly. Stepping back to examine oneself from a distance is not just helpful, but essential.

Some people try to hide their past and, hell, in my case there would be a lot to hide. The analysing process was painful, but I did not stop until all the skeletons in the cupboard had come out. Boy, they did look ugly, and all of them with my own face! Had I really been this selfish, bitchy person? There was no denying it. When I asked my best friend why she never told me, she replied: "*You would not have listened anyway.*" She was right. To have a rich and complex inner life can be an advantage, but it is not always pleasant.

## Reflection on 'anxious' Introverts

It is described that *"anxious introverts avoid socialising because they feel awkward and painfully self-conscious around other people."* Also, *"this type of introversion is defined by a tendency to ruminate."*

(Jenn Granneman. March 10, 2015. Introvert, Dear. Retrieved from https://introvertdear.com/news/science-says-there-are-4-kinds-of-introverts)

Well, in my case, that depends on the people I meet. See, I don't know anyone at the farmers' market around the corner. Yet I don't feel awkward to speak or joke with them at all. When accompanied by friends, they often asked me if I know these people. They were astonished to learn that I did not and said: *"You seemed so familiar with them."* My mother was the same, but my daughter does not go to the market at all. Neither is she fond of talking to anyone she is unfamiliar with.

There are situations, though, when I feel *self-conscious* around others. Usually, that happens when I am surrounded by or confronted with people I don't gel with. Aside from my main job as an IT specialist, I am a healer by nature and educated in it as well. As such, I can sense and read auras. I don't see them, but I receive their energy structure. Then, my mind transforms the auras into mental pictures. You could say that I can sense and see a person's essence quite clearly. I don't even need to see people in reality. It also works via phone or with a picture. Possibly, it has got to do with the fact that on the spiritual level, we all are connected. So, when I am confronted with a person who does not like me, I just know it. This should give me an advantage instead of making me feel self-conscious, right? Strangely enough, it does not, and it annoys me.

Five years ago, I began to develop a strategy for situations when the resonance systems of others bother me. Using my imagination, I visualize myself protected within three levels of healing energy. The first one is a cocoon of white light (Light). This is enclosed by a second one: a light-blue octahedron (Magic). The two of them float in a lucent, golden globe (Love).

While doing it, I chant in my mind the words *"I am Light, Magic, and Love. I am Strength, Power, and Wisdom. I am the Music and the Word."* It does not take long to counterbalance the other resonance systems. Then, all is well again. In fact, it is an act of choosing: a part of my inner vibration potential I want to activate.

There are other revealing aspects about introversion. *"An anxious introvert may turn things over and over in their mind, wondering what could have, or what already has gone wrong. They may have trouble shutting off their obsessive negative thoughts. They may even stay awake, late at night, playing events over and over in their mind."*

(Jenn Granneman. March 10, 2015. Introvert, Dear. Retrieved from https://introvertdear.com/news/science-says-there-are-4-kinds-of-introverts)

That sounds familiar. It haunted me for years. Eventually, I began using a remarkably helpful technique called *Transcendental Meditation* ™. I will return to this part in another chapter. In any case, I would describe socialising in general as a minefield of potential hazards that I'd rather avoid entering.

## Reflection on 'restrained' Introverts

Again, I'd like to quote Jenn Granneman: *"Restrained introverts tend to operate at a slightly slower pace. They may take a while to get going. They prefer to think before they speak or act. To relax, they like to slow down and take it easy, as opposed to seeking out new or exciting experiences and sensations. They may sometimes feel sluggish and lacking energy. "*

(Jenn Granneman. March 10, 2015. Introvert, Dear. Retrieved from https://introvertdear.com/news/science-says-there-are-4-kinds-of-introverts)

The topic is becoming more and more interesting! My mother might be partly a restrained introvert. She always thoroughly thought things through before speaking, with the usual exceptions, of course. Sometimes, our temper gets the better of us. The same applies to my daughter. Because of her reserved nature, she also takes her time to make decisions and to get ready, which drives me crazy at times. You probably already suspect that this might not entirely apply to me.

As soon as I could speak I did so extensively. Legend has it that I could do it before I was born, babbling in my mother's womb. Later, there were even suggestions to seal my lips with plaster. It was that bad! So, there was no way I took more time than necessary to think about what I wanted to say. I did think, very fast, but my impatient nature had its limits and still does. When I got myself in trouble with that, another part of my sanguine temper came in handy: an uncanny skill to interpolate. In other words, I could talk myself out of nearly everything without delay. Often, I realized my mistakes even before a sentence ended. Thus, I could turn the tide in time.

Regarding my person, *restrained* is not the first word that comes to mind, not even the last one. Taking a slower pace is good advice, though. Until five years ago, I did not even know what that was. On the contrary, as far as I remember, I always was a driven person. The motives behind this behaviour might have been the urge to win and to get approval. Whatever the matter, I needed to be faster than anyone. Even when I was alone, I acted no differently. It was as if I had to prove it to myself. Strict education by my father was another aspect. He always pushed his children to give their best and to be the best. For him, there was no other way, and we thought it was the only right one.

As every wise person experiences at some point, destiny has a nasty habit of intervening, if we don't see reason otherwise. In my life, this happened not just once. One day, I had private harp lessons at my home. My gentle, patient teacher M. is a brilliant musician in general and very skilled in playing harp and guitar.

He wanted to accompany me on the guitar, so I clambered up to the loft to get one. At least I thought it was there (it wasn't). Well, clambered is not the proper word here. I must rather have rushed upstairs, head over heels. That was when I missed the last step. I don't remember anything about this moment because my lights went out immediately, and I collapsed upstairs on top of my hands. Apparently, my head had collided with a shelf, and I had blacked out.

After regaining consciousness, the pain in my head and hands told me that something must have been broken. By the time I got to the hospital, a few very wicked looking bruises were spreading over my face. The doctor, of course, immediately considered me a victim of domestic abuse, which I clearly was not. Fortunately, nothing was broken, but a mild concussion explained why my thinking had slowed down somewhat.

That incident got me thinking. My guardian angels must have tried to deliver the message that it is time to slow down things a bit. Jetting through life like a comet as I did obviously was a dangerous thing to do. Suffice it to write that I took their advice seriously. From that moment on, I made it a rule to slow down important things such as walking, eating, and thinking. It was a conscious decision and had nothing to do with me becoming a *restrained* introvert. It still goes against the grain of my nature, but I manage. Many good things came out of it.

Now, let's take a closer look at the statement: "*Some of them can't, for instance, wake up and immediately spring into action.*"

(Melissa Dahl. August 11, 2020. The Cut. Apparently There Are 4 Kinds of Introversion. Retrieved from: https://www.thecut.com/article/apparently-there-are-four-kinds-of-introversion.html)

Take my daughter. She likes nothing more than to take her time for everything. This already showed in her early childhood. When she was in the middle of playing with her toys and I told her it is time for supper, she blanched and protested resolutely. There was no way to convince her, and every time she wheedled an extension out of me with pleading eyes. For my daughter, this wasn't a game or faked excuse. I could tell that she was on the brink of panic, so I needed to come up with another tactic.

It had started as a battle of wills, but eventually turned into a habit of reminding her three times before supper. Apart from the last time, she insisted on my confirmation that there was still time left for playing. Amazingly, this trick worked. One might think that my daughter's behaviour had changed by now. Far from it! We still have the same problem. The difference is that now, I don't expect her to be on time anymore. I have learned to respect her special nature and now know better than telling her to get her skates on.

54

As for my mother with her large family, she was kind of forced to wake up and immediately spring into action. She did not have a choice. Otherwise, she would never have been able to manage everything as smoothly as she did. Later, when all her children lived abroad, my mother loved to linger in bed for a while after waking up. Otherwise, she was a person who did not hesitate, whenever she wanted to get things done.

The same applies to me. I am a very active person, so I needed to develop the habit of planning my breaks more carefully. My body has shown me several times how important it is to keep a balance between tension and relaxation. Everything takes its time, so I had to learn to curb my impatience.

## Thoughts on 'willed' Introverts

After reading about the four types of introverts mentioned above, I wasn't yet satisfied with their variety of categories. There must be more. Suddenly, a realisation hit home. Somehow, I had brought to a certain degree of perfection consciously using traits of introversion to my advantage. Now, I see them as tools to deliberately enhance my life.

In the chapter *Pitfall Groups and Network,* I describe myself as a kind of chameleon. Spot-on, because depending on its surroundings, the chameleon changes its appearance consciously. This way, I am using the assets of introversion willingly to blend in. Escaping other people's nosiness and keeping them from prying into my private life are two of the benefits. It also enables me to choose my words carefully when I turn down invitations. There is just a thin line between being honest and appearing rude. To reject things, I am not willing to do or say, is essential for my well-being. Many people seem to have problems to do that. They have a guilty conscience when they say "*No*" to others, so as not to put their own welfare above social obligations.

Guess what I stumbled over when I had nearly finished this book? A quotation from *Joseph Campbell's* book *The Hero with a Thousand Faces* caught my attention:

*"Willed introversion, in fact, is one of the classic implements of creative genius and can be employed as a deliberate device. It drives the psychic energies into depth and activates the lost continent of unconscious infantile and archetypal images. If the personality is able to absorb and integrate the new forces, there will be experienced an almost superhuman degree of self-consciousness and masterful control."*

(Joseph Campbell. "n.d.". The Hero With a Thousand Faces. Goodreads. Quotable Quotes. Retrieved from: https://www.goodreads.com/quotes/8874787-willed-introversion-in-fact-is-one-of-the-classic-implements)

It hits the bull's eye because this is exactly how I experience it: *self-consciousness and masterful control.* That is, introversion could be compared to an armoury of extremely viable devices. One just needs to learn to utilize them accordingly. We talk about courage, power, and wisdom here.

Meanwhile, I have grown into a confident introvert, but I don't consider it as a withdrawal from the world. I see it as fully embracing the virtues I have been blessed with. Talents we don't develop and use are wasted gifts. Still, it took me many years to overcome the insecurities of my childhood days.

My father had set very high standards in every way, making us believe they applied to the whole world. Only later, I discovered they did not. He certainly loved us, but we children lived in constant fear of failing. What if we would not be able to live up to his standards? Knowing nothing about introversion prevented me from acknowledging my true nature. We have been trained to obey. Rarely, we dared to trust the value or accuracy of our own thoughts and conclusions.

Performing the transformation from a subconscious introvert to a willed introvert was a huge improvement. It did not happen overnight, but took at least 15 years of trial and error. As established before, we of introverted nature need time for contemplating and planning. To recalibrate one's inculcated behaviour is the hardest thing, but footprints on the sands of time are not made by sitting down. So, I was bound to bite the bullet at some point.

Studying *Joseph Campbell's* books about mythology, I realised once more that these insights are not new to us. He refers to ancient knowledge, skilfully woven into myths and legends all over the world. Whenever I am reading Fairy tales from different countries, it occurs to me that their essences and messages are basically the same. Their analogies are unmistakable and exciting.

I like the thought that an all embracing wisdom is enclosed in the entirety of stories spanning the whole world: the most valuable treasure ever. Perhaps, some people just don't pay enough attention to the hidden messages of myths or might not be able to identify them as such. Maybe, they assume that myths are for children only. Children absorb the truth of Fairy tales subconsciously, whereas adults can add the traits of consciousness. Then, we have come full circle.

# Disguised amidst Extroverts

I n this chapter, I muse about awkward situations introverts find themselves in. Again, I am contemplating several aspects from *Jenn Granneman's* website, reflecting if and how this applies to members of my family.

## Strangers in a Crowd

*"You often feel lonelier in a crowd than when you're alone. There's something about being with a group that makes you feel disconnected from yourself. Maybe it's because it's hard to hear your inner voice when there's so much noise around you. Or maybe you feel like another, like I did. Whatever the reason, as an introvert, you crave intimate moments and deep connections — and those usually aren't found in a crowd."*

(Jenn Granneman. March 10, 2015. Introvert, Dear. Retrieved from https://introvertdear.com/news/science-says-there-are-4-kinds-of-introverts)

I could not have put it better. The three of us always hated being in crowds. It is not just that we don't need it, we despise it. Instead, we prefer to decide for ourselves what to think and to do. Crowds have the tendency to spoil that. They develop a sort of momentum that moves in the wrong direction. Groups don't like it when individuals go against the grain. The latter is just what we like best, for we love to think and to get to the bottom of things instead of enduring the meaningless chatter of people in crowds.

With time, one can learn not to feel disconnected from oneself in a crowd. How is the saying? *Disappointment grows with your expectation*. Thus, it is better to expect nothing or at least to know what can be anticipated. Meanwhile, I even feel protected by a crowd if nobody takes notice of me or talks to me. To make myself invisible amongst people is a skill that pays to be nurtured. Loud people tend to overlook the quiet ones anyway, which works to our advantage.

Acceptance of things that cannot be changed is another quality that helps me to cope. Otherwise, I would never be able to stand crowds at concerts I attend now and then. There, they are a necessary evil, so to speak. In a concert hall, the situation is different, where everyone is confined to their seats and unlikely to get in my way unexpectedly.

After the concerts, one is either faster in leaving than the crowd is or just sits it out.

There is another thing I have never got used to and maybe never will. At noon, I need a warm meal for lunch. This is important because this is my main meal. Ideally, I'd like to eat alone in a quiet corner, preferably at home. In my case, this is impossible, except from the times I can work in my home office. My only option is the cafeteria, and that is the problem. There, I cannot escape the chitter-chatter, the inevitable noise and my colleagues' curious looks when I unpack my food. If I could, I just would make the people disappear.

The even better option would be a magical cloak of invisibility. I can't tell you how many times I've wished for that. Now that I write down this story, the COVID-19 pandemic is still in full swing. It might sound strange, but I am in my element right now. Working at home gives me exactly what I want.

While I am writing about the cloak of invisibility, another memory bubbles up to the surface. There are only few occasions when I feel safe and comfortable outside my home. The first one is when at 5.30 in the morning, I leave for the office. It is beyond words how beautiful my town is without any people milling about. Undisturbed, the ancient buildings and towers stand proudly amidst the fascinating kaleidoscope of light and shadow. Sometimes, their patterns remind me of runes. After the bird's dawn chorus has stilled, silence is but a lull, settling everywhere. In winter, leafless trees reveal dark blotches against a shimmering sky: the empty nests of last summer's rookery. Alas, nothing lasts forever, because all too soon the unbearable noise of the first cars moving about brutally destroys my silent contemplation.

Another occasion is when I am walking alone, with a close friend or with my daughter. Usually, we are so focused on each other that everything appears to be tuned out completely. In that situation, I am not aware of other people at all or of them looking at me. There are no words to describe how I loathe it when people stare at me. In my book, there is nothing to stare at. I am neither ugly nor beautiful, but something draws them to me like a magnet. My friends claim it to be my powerful aura, which is possible.

Yes, of course, there is another story behind that observation. One summer day, my beautiful daughter and I were walking hand in hand through the quiet city. She must have been 22 years old, then. After we had talked about something pleasant, we enjoyed each other's company in silence, smiling. It was when a middle-aged woman passed by, looking at us in an amused, curious way. Normally, I would never have addressed her directly. But I wanted to know why she was looking at us like that. *"What is it?"* I asked bluntly. Her smile deepened, and she said: *"I could not help it, but the two of you look so lovely together and so deeply connected. It is beautiful."* I was so stunned that I forgot to reply altogether. My daughter and I did not stop smiling until we reached her home. So, it wasn't that bad, or was it?

As for people staring at me, - I also dislike it when they look into the rooms of my flat. Sometimes, when it is dark outside, pictures of neighbours, peeping through my windows with long-distance cameras, flash through the back of my mind. Does this sound ridiculous? In my case, it is a bit difficult to put up blinds, for I live under the roof eaves, where most of the windows are not rectangular.

That is not the worst thing, though. Every night when I pull up the roller blinds, I am confronted with a most unappetizing view. In the house across the yard where one of the apartments is worth about 600.000 Euros, people don't bother with curtains on their windows. There is no problem with that unless it gets ugly, and it does, at least in one case. In summer, one man obviously seems to find it appropriate to sprawl every evening in his lounger with wide-spread legs, dressed in underpants. There is only one word that comes to mind: disgusting.

Am I misanthropic because I go along with *Jean-Paul Sartre,* who said that "*Hell is other people.*"? Especially at breakfast, if I may say so... Sometimes, I find other people not just tiring, but also irritating. As mentioned before, when I am on holiday I prefer to rent an apartment or house rather than stay in a hotel. The latter is a real nuisance. Not only are they overpriced, but you pay to be regularly disturbed in your room. Plus, the space is quite limited. It does not feel cosy either, and the worst happens in the mornings. Breakfast with other people is hell indeed. They check out what you are wearing, how you are walking, whom you are sharing a table with, what you have on your plate, and how many times you go to the buffet. And they just don't shut up! That's horrific!

However, the things listed here don't bother my daughter as much, simply because she mostly tunes out of what others around her are doing. Neither is she interested in what they might think about her. Thanks to her sub-conscious, which apparently provides for a selective perception, she simply doesn't per-ceive most of these things at all. My daughter is more annoyed by the noise around her (which is much harder to tune out) and the fact that strangers have zero respect for so-called personal space. Is it too much to ask to keep a certain minimum distance? Ironically, with the enforced social distancing right now, the pandemic proves to be useful again.

## Pitfall Groups and Network

Let's find out if working in groups is a curse or a blessing for our 'Spiritual Trinity'.

Jenn wrote: "You feel like you're faking it when you have to network. Walking up to strangers and introducing yourself? You'd rather stick tiny needles under your fingernails. But you know there's value in it, so you might do it anyway – except you feel like a phony the entire time. You might have read self-help books about how to be a better conversationalist or exude more charisma. In the moment, you must activate your "public persona." You might say things to yourself like, "Smile, make eye contact, and use your loud-confident voice!" Then, when you're finished, you feel beat, and you need downtime to recover. You wonder, - does everyone else have to try this hard when meeting new people?"

(Jenn Granneman. March 10, 2015. Introvert, Dear. Retrieved from https://introvertdear.com/news/science-says-there-are-4-kinds-of-introverts)

Hmm, what our 'Spiritual Trinity' has in common is that we don't like it when we must introduce ourselves to strangers. My hunch is that we will never get used to it as much as we try. It has become one of these bad habits in companies that everyone needs to introduce oneself to a group. My voice is always thick with fear when it is my turn. In such moments, I just wish the earth to swallow me up. There is no explanation for that. By now, I have worked more than 30 years in teams, and I am very good at what I do. There is no reason why I would feel so self-conscious and awkward every time I need to introduce myself. It possibly has got to do with the fact that many people stare pointedly at me. I tell you what: I am so looking forward to my retirement!

No, not everyone has to try so hard when meeting new people. Extroverts are experts in introducing themselves. They even tell you things nobody wants to know about! We could learn a lot from them, but I prefer to stay an introverted person. I am sure that my difficulties have nothing to do with my abilities to communicate. We will come to that part later.

Networking has never been a problem for me, although I am the perfect loner. Leave me alone in a room without any disturbances, and I am twice as much prolific and efficient as in an open-plan office. That is what the management doesn't get. There have been many published studies and statistics about different kinds of working conditions for introverted and extroverted people. They came up with the same results. Extroverts need groups for working efficiently, and introverts need to work in isolation for better results. Is this so hard to understand? No, that is not the problem. The money and control are. People in open-plan offices are easier to be observed. Plus, single rooms are more expensive. What the management doesn't take into account is that open office environments undermine creative productivity. In doing so, they also discriminate against non-extroverts. By the way, open-plan offices are the perfect places to transmit viruses quickly and securely...

Anyway, despite being an introvert, I am the perfect team worker, believe it or not. It must be one of these many talents I have been blessed with from the very beginning. Sometimes it amuses me when my colleagues think I am an extroverted person because I am so good at communication. Whereas I would be a dodgy movie star in front of a camera, I am a decent actress in real life. It is not that I pretend to be a person I am not. The funny thing is that I am all these different characters indeed.

A few years ago, I talked to my lifelong friend K. about my suspicion to consist of at least three personalities, which made her laugh and got me thinking. Two years later, my Scottish friend I. made an Astro Chart for me and said: *"Be aware that you have very strong, totally different energies which would mean that sometimes these themes act out totally as if they are the dominant energy, and do not seem to easily communicate with the other strong themes in your chart. As I said, it is almost as if you have 3/4 different personalities in there, and at times one will want to be in control without the others, and you would not usually be aware of this happening, maybe up until now when you have been made aware of this dynamic."*

My great advantage is that of being like a chameleon. Whenever needed, I can switch smoothly into either introversion- or extroversion-mode. When working in a group, my heightened senses make it possible to capture the general mood easily. This enables me to offer compromises long before any of the others became aware of a pending conflict. Also, my ability to read between the lines, interpreting unspoken words, comes in handy.

Another underlying aspect of my personality is that I never lose my focus on a goal. If necessary, I subordinate myself. That does not mean I hold back with my opinion or shy away from confrontations. I am a fighter, after all.

When it comes to *sports*, there are many choices. You just need to find the right one. My mother and my daughter were hardly active in sports. But my youngest sister and I were top athletes for many years. The advantage of being a swimmer is that, although a member of a team, one can do one's training relatively undisturbed. In the water, you are on your own. Save from the moments of breathing in, everyone needs to keep one's mouth shut. While I swam along the lanes, either leisurely or sprinting, there was a lot of time for thinking, which always was one of my favourite pastimes. Of course, we were supposed to pay attention to our swim style at any time. But honestly, who can concentrate solely on that during a 3-hours training session? After my heydays of swimming and as a true sanguine person, I indulged in a variety of other sports, such as shooting, diving, judo, and volleyball. None of these sports was a problem for me as an introvert, for they did not require much talking or socializing.

One of the most beautiful hobbies is diving. For safety reasons, we were not allowed to dive without a partner, and only after months of training and numerous tests. I don't know if everyone experiences diving as I did, but it is just awesome. Under water, everything is slow, quiet, and outright beautiful. Moving in slow motion is just marvellous. Quite often, I found myself unwilling to return to the surface and the noisy world beyond.

Diving reminds me of a recurrent dream of my childhood. Nearly every night, I dreamed of diving without any equipment. As soon as I was underwater, the skin beneath my ears opened, and gills were pumping oxygen into my lungs. At first, I was sceptical that it would work, but when I opened my mouth to let water in, I could breathe! I could breathe indeed! What a wonder and pleasure! Alas, as soon as I had surfaced from my dream and touched my skin, the spell was broken.

74

I was downright devastated. Rarely in my life have I been happier than during those diving hours in dreams I did not want to wake up from. In 2017, when I attended a 'Poetry Course' at *Moniack Mhor*, Scotland's Creative Writing Centre amidst the breath-taking Scottish Highlands, I wrote a poem about that dream.

About 10 years ago, I came across another fascinating sport that enabled me to balance the thin line between spending time with a group and the never-ceasing need to be alone. One day, I saw a picture on a website of young people fencing with each other.

## Breath Taking

*Gills, white, fragile gills*
*Right behind my ears*
*That is what I dreamed of*
*Since my childhood days*
*It set me free in a way*
*Nothing else would*

*Is it foolish that wish*
*To never arise again from*
*This magnificent vicinity*
*Beneath the surface of*
*Healing audible silence?*

*Agravic is how I feel*
*Happy is what I am*
*Strange is what I hear*
*Breath taking is what I see*

*What a perfect world*
*Of chosen solitude*
*Outbalanced and quiet*
*In its true natural setting*

ISIS (2017)

This triggered another one of my fondest childhood memories. In summer, I liked to craft bows, arrows and wooden swords. My romantic nature and unflagging spirit drove me to hours of fighting against visible and invisible foes. Interestingly, I was never fond of playing a helpless, boring princess, waiting at the battlements for her cavaliers. It went without saying that I was the Knight in shining armour!

First, I did not know that it was possible to train in historical martial arts in Germany. But as soon as my interest was aroused, I searched for the best fencing masters in Germany and contacted one of them: *Sven Baumgarten*. He had made it his calling and profession to train people in historical martial arts. Sven is one of these few persons who you want to surround yourself with. He proved to be a fantastic teacher as well as a skilled fighter. Alas, his fencing school was too far away. Otherwise I could have been trained there regularly. Fortunately, there were many weekend courses, and so my journey to become a fencer began.

If there was one who could show me the ropes, it was gentle, patient Sven. Boy, - was it hard to learn that, and I am not just talking about physical matters. The swords are said to be the weapons of the spirit and for a reason. After 9 hours of intensive training, one's mind feels unbearably tired because there is so much to pay attention to. You don't just have to coordinate your own legs, arms, and the rest of your body. One also needs to watch every tiny movement of one's opponent very closely. Otherwise, you are dead, figuratively spoken. Plus, it is beneficial if you can remember the technique your trainer showed you a few minutes ago, which gets harder as time goes on. At some point, muscles and brain outright refuse to cooperate, but you need to overcome these moments. Speaking of will-power and endurance...

Had not I loved fencing so much, I might have given up because there was a downside to it. The courses have been attended by many people who did not know each other. Very often, one was supposed to fence with a person who you had not picked yourself for a partner. In hindsight, I see it as a character-building procedure, but I never got used to it. Some men thought they needed to prove what brutes they can be, throwing caution to the winds. It was one of the seminar's rules to be considerate and that we take care of each other. Not everyone got the message, though. This bothered me the most. Also, I found it awkward to sit with the attendees in one room during the breaks. Many of them were introverts too.

Nonetheless, a few times I joined Sven, his family, and other fencers in the yearly 'Sword-fighting Holidays' at *Erchless Castle*, near *Inverness* in the *Scottish Highlands*. This was another tough challenge and compromise regarding operating in a group full of strangers. In the end, my romantic nature overruled the introverted part of me. There is nothing like fencing on beautiful castle grounds under tall, ancient trees in perfect silence. Only the cattle and sheep were watching, while lazily cropping grass.

Sometimes, we drove through the breath-taking Scottish Highlands and paused at romantic spots for fencing. We favoured bridges, hills and waterfalls. Once we encountered a bagpiper wandering along the ridge of a brae playing beautiful melodies. I remember wishing I could walk with him for a while. The mountains, hills and music would be enough for me.

Apart from that, however, there were also many things that worked against the grain of my introversion. It began with me being an intrinsic 'early bird' who needs lunch at 11.30, dead on time. Training started late, so it was not finished before 13.30. Not good. Afterwards, there was barely time for changing clothes before we went on a trip. No time for warm lunch either and getting worse. Supper was not ready before 20.00, which is the time I usually go to bed. Unthinkable, aside from the fact that my stomach doesn't digest anything eaten after 17.30! So, things went out of the frying pan and into the fire.

The next problem was sharing a room with another person. The alternative, though, was too costly. Even when I had managed to go to bed at 10 p.m., my later retiring roommate regularly woke me up at midnight, which made falling asleep impossible for the next two hours. After two days, I felt ill and completely drained of energy. Maybe, I had turned into one of the castle's ghosts, who knows?

So the consequence of this was that I needed another 5 leave days to replenish my reserves afterwards. Each time, I swore that I would never repeat these fencing holidays in Scotland. You guess it already: I caved in for another four times... Well, at least there was one nice benefit. Afterwards, in complete solitude at home, I created photo books from pictures of Scotland's breath-taking beauty.

## Sound of the Swords

*Silently the world dissolves*
*Behind a curtain of oblivion*
*Nimble feet shift gently*
*To the sounds of Swords*
*Like Strikes of lightning*

*Vital moments of awareness*
*Slightest motions, fully observed*
*By dancers in perilous circles*
*Graceful movements become*
*Barely hidden entrapments*

*Always alert, eyes are locked*
*Black masks conceal emotions*
*Bending, stretching, leaping forwards*
*Bodies bow like weeping willows*
*Until the blades are clashing*

*Invisible, through pulsing veins*
*Heat unfurls in waves of fire*
*Spirits soar high in their purity:*
*Absolved from martial reasons*
*Offenders and defenders alike*

ISIS (2016)

## Dodging the Limelight

Oh yes! I am so bent on dodging the limelight that it can appear paranoid at times. I don't know about my mother, but as children, my daughter and I were not keen at shooting up our hands in class at all. The teachers always tried to get us to participate more actively, but usually we found the attention that came with it too uncomfortable. Now and then, one needed to do it to steer clear of unsatisfying markings, though.

All my testimonies had one thing in common, namely that I should keep my mouth shut during the lessons. Of course, I didn't because I couldn't. Communicating was essential for me at any time and in any place. My teachers just never understood how boring it was to listen to the same sermon over and over again. Nothing has changed aside from the fact that nowadays, most of the time I manage to keep my mouth shut in meetings. Even if I know the answer, I tend to let others bask in the limelight. I no longer feel the need to prove anything to anyone, for now I know who I am and what I am capable of. That's enough. Yet, there are situations, when I prefer one-on-one conversations with my boss, because I hate to discuss particular topics with the whole team.

The degrees of maturity of my colleagues are very different, so talking with them would just end in fruitless discussions I refuse to waste my precious energy for. True, when I feel passionate about something, I might let myself get carried away, which usually ends in a fiasco. Afterwards, I swear never to do this again. So far, I have failed to keep my promise. But I refuse to give up trying. This goes without saying.

Dodging the limelight also shows in the fact that I don't like it *to be praised in public*. Even when my boss compliments me in a one on one interview, I can barely stand it. With my friends it is different. I have learned to accept their praise gracefully, even thanking them, and I feel good afterwards.

Most likely, I will never *perform a concert* with my harp. But I am trying to train myself to play in public places, just for fun (not for money). At times when the churches are mostly empty, I play there for an hour or so. Normally, I would never do such a thing. However, these vaulted high ceilings create a unique acoustic, which draws me in. Although I am not a believer, in gothic churches I can feel the mighty power of the Holy Spirit. It encourages me to achieve things that reach far beyond me. Also, it is healing and helps me overcome my aversion to being exposed to the public.

Then, there is *writing*. Together with my Twin Soul OSIRIS, I have published several books of poems. Whereas an extrovert would thrive on the attention of the public, I can't stand it. That is, I would never use my real name. Without a pseudonym, it would be impossible for me to publish anything. The mere thought of being dragged into the limelight makes me want to die.

For me, publishing a book is not about becoming rich or famous. Poems and stories are works of art. They are offers to the world and will find those people who are looking for them. It does not matter whether there are millions or just five people who like my writing. Works of art are for the artist as blossoms are to a tree. In quiet moments, I see myself as an old solitary tree. Standing tall in a meadow of flowers: my thoughts and written words become blown-away blossoms. Before I know, they are gone with the wind and get caught in the hair of unsuspecting wanderers.

Sometimes, one could get the impression that in this strange, new world, everything is still about connections, being in the limelight, or a bestseller author. I have been reading many bestseller books. To tell the truth, a few of them I did not enjoy or even stopped reading. So what does it tell us? Exactly, - that all of this means nothing if the writing is not to the reader's taste, no matter how highly the book is praised.

Many good writers never get the chance to publish anything because they don't have the right connections. That is why I encourage self-publishing. This allows readers to choose from a much larger pool of books. As an author, you can write a book without being pressed for time by a publisher. Besides, print on demand is much better for our environment.

## Solitude Intrusions

Solitude intrusions come in manifold disguise. Not all of them can be evaded easily. When I thought about *Jenn Granneman's* extroverted friend, who is always calling her when she's alone in the car, I became aware that I have no such friends. Isn't that wonderful? Yes, but those are not the only *phone calls* spoiling solitude.

In my life, it happens very rarely that someone calls me at an inconvenient time. My friends and I have an agreement. We always make appointments for phone calls via email, out of respect for the other one's tight schedule. Another reason is the fact that when they happen, our calls last for at least one or two hours. Most important: we don't chat, but talk. Many a decent topic comes up in our conversations. That is why we like to take our time and don't want to be under pressure.

In the past, when someone called me at an inconvenient time, I felt guilty for not picking up the receiver, so I took the call. Afterwards, I was annoyed with myself for not having refused it. Over time, I changed my attitude considerably. You might deem it rude, but when it happens now, I don't take the call anymore, at least not when it is inconvenient. People know very well that they can leave a message on my answering machine. This way, I can decide, if, and when to call back.

My daughter has adapted this habit too and sticks to it, no matter what. That's my girl! As for my mother, she did not have to fight such battles because most of her life, she simply did not have a phone. Only during her last 10 years or so, she possessed one. Then, it was more of a pleasure because she was retired and had enough time to spare. Besides, she loved to talk with her children and grandchildren.

*Showing up* at my house without an invitation is another intrusion I consider preposterous. If I don't expect anyone, I just keep quiet in my sacred space and don't answer the door. In my only haven, I feel safe, and I hate to be ambushed.

Other kinds of intrusion come in the shape of *invitations to parties*. How I hate them! People who know me well enough, would never think of inviting me to a party or another kind of gathering. Obviously, my distaste for invitations showed very early. From the very beginning, I refused to host any birthday parties. The bright side of it was that I have not been invited to other kids' parties either. Interestingly, no one ever remarked on it, although I am quite sure that there was a lot of talking behind my back going on. Maybe, they have been afraid of me, which was possibly very wise. My choleric temper is nothing to be trifled with, although it has mellowed a bit over the years.

Since 2019, I also disposed of the habit of giving and receiving presents on occasions like birthdays and so on. Isn't it dreadful to feel the pressure of buying a gift for a person who has got everything already? Hence, my friends and I agreed upon stopping this tradition altogether. Of course, there are always exceptions. It is still allowed to give each other presents if they come our way perchance. The funny thing is that when I talked with my friends about it, each and every one of them was kind of relieved because they had felt the same for years. Sometimes, it just takes one person to say it out loud, and everything changes.

If I remember correctly, my mother did host her own birthday parties only within the close family. My daughter never did anything of this sort. Like me, she was not interested in celebrating with other people, save from her boyfriend and me. Of course, I suggested it every year as she matured and felt just a tiny bit guilty for being relieved when she refused.

Last year, I became aware of another kind of solitude killer. To work on this book in peace and silence, I thought it a good idea to rent my friends' beach house at beautiful *Lake Constance* on the *Isle of Reichenau*. Weeks before, I imagined spending most of the time at the private beach, listening leisurely to the *"lake water lapping with low sounds by the shore"* (William Butler Yeats, 'The Lake Isle of Innisfree'). We have had such a warm, sunny September, and the lake was still warm enough for swimming. I was looking forward to watching the wading birds and boats dancing on the waves, and surely it would be a writer's paradise. Usually, I steer clear of any expectations. But this time, I could not help myself, because I was so excited to finally have the time and perfect surroundings to write, or so I thought.

What can I say? When I arrived, I was quite relaxed and in a good mood. By the time I left the beach house after a fortnight, I felt angry and unsettled. The only quiet times were the early morning hours and late evening when the tourists were gone. When the stars appeared on the black velvet canvas, I just marvelled at them, totally at ease.

Nature and my accommodation were perfect. My friends had done everything to make the house and garden a comfortable, cosy home. The view over the blue lake was outright spectacular. Sitting under the 500 years old black poplar tree: dining, musing or stargazing was a real vision. What was the problem then? As usual, it was the people. Unfortunately, a narrow pathway runs between the private beach and the garden, - a fact I had not been aware of when I rented the house. Every two minutes or so, chatting people walked by. The worst thing was that they stuck their nosy faces through the hedges of the property, although there were 'Private' signs everywhere. It was unbearable. I felt like an ape in the zoo.

Initially, I went to this place to have my privacy and got quite the opposite. A few times, I even had to fend off insolent sailors or swimmers, who thought they could occupy my private beach as if it was their own. It was even more annoying when I was disturbed by them while trying to doze after lunch.

As if this would not be enough, the neighbour's house was under construction. For about ten hours a day, there was not a minute without noises: scraping, drilling, hammering or sawing. When the machines finally had stilled, children started screaming and shouting. My soul was suffering in silence. Not once in my lifetime, I have experienced such noisy holidays and ironically in one of the most beautiful places in the world.

Inside the house, it was different. Embraced by its peaceful aura, I felt sheltered and safe. From my favoured chair at the table, I could see the lake in front of me as well as the glorious, black poplar. To my right, I enjoyed the glamorous sun rising in a spotless sky, whereas to my left breath-taking, purple sunsets rendered me speechless.

Primarily, I wanted to work undisturbed on my book, because at home, one gets distracted by lots of things on the task list. Also, I had hoped the surrounding nature to be a kind of inspiration. The day before my departure, I considered whether I should return to this place one day. It wasn't easy, but in the end, I decided against it. If I need to stay inside to write in solitude, I might as well do it in my own home. Suddenly, I realized that my flat is the perfect place to think and write undisturbed indeed. Sometimes one has to travel to come to such a conclusion.

## Dreams of joint Solitude

*Gone: black covers of the silent night*
*As crystal stars were scattered wide*
*Heaven watched the earth till dawn*
*As morning's glory clad the lawn*

*Fanning out her flashing rays*
*The sun rose in abundant grace*
*Beams of healing light remained*
*Celestial beauty we never gained*

*Would that we walk in forest's glade*
*Hands entwined, in wattles' shade*
*Bravely we would hold back tears*
*Unspoken words dissolved the fears*

*Precious moments of joint solitude*
*Mingled with the west-wind's mood*
*Hearts: aglow with everlasting shine*
*That emanates from our love divine*

*The new-born, quiet morning grew*
*Where rivulets through chasms flew*
*Like our hopes and heartfelt dreams*
*Becoming torrents out of streams*

ISIS (2016)

## The Matter of Small Talk

The pleasure of *small talk* is a matter of one's point of view. Extroverts almost revel in it. Our '*Spiritual Trinity*' tries to avoid and escape it whenever possible. I have never seen my mother small-talking. Maybe, she was forced into it during the breaks between the school lessons, when she was a teacher. This reminds me of having heard that she volunteered often for supervising the pupils. I always wondered why anyone would want to do this. But in retrospect, it might have been the lesser evil for her. Back then, it was still allowed to smoke in the teachers' lounge, and my mother loathed it.

Also, we are guilty of hiding away when people who we'd rather avoid talking with, walk towards us. The same goes for neighbours we hear in the hallway. We barely know each other and don't want to intensify the contact more than necessary. My daughter and I have developed this tactic nearly to the point of perfection, I think. Occasionally, we get caught, though. It comes from not moving fast enough (anymore). There you are. In any case, avoidance is better than small talk.

It does not just happen in our homes, but on the market, in shops and everywhere else in public too. My daughter and I have an advantage here. We moved into town about 16 years ago, and are proud to admit to have barely made knew acquaintances since then. Most of our colleagues live in distant villages. This is very helpful when walking through the city.

*"We'd rather talk about something meaningful than fill the air with chatter just to hear ourselves make noise. We find small talk inauthentic, and, frankly, many of us feel awkward doing it."*

(Jenn Granneman. December 22, 2018. Introverts, Psychology. Retrieved from https://tppahanshilhorst. Wordpress.com/ tag/focus/)

Quite right, Jenn! We cannot bear pointless chatter for long. It is so much more pleasant to sit with a close friend, engrossed in serious discussions. Our energy levels get boosted, and we feel deeply satisfied. Conversations of this kind are not possible with everyone. Talking with extroverts often leaves us drained and tired.

Aside from not liking small talk, I am surprisingly skilled at it. Chameleon-like, I can switch into chatty-mode any time necessary to spell-bind my torturers with words they haven't even heard of. There are times when it is a real pleasure to enmesh them in a net of words to lead them on paths by my own will. In the beginning, it was a sheer nuisance to dodge every uncomfortable question, because it depletes one's well of energy faster than in a blink of an eye.

At some point, I began to use the extroverts' weaknesses to my advantage. They like nothing more than to talk about themselves. Excellent! So, the best thing to do is fire one question after the other in their direction. Should they get in one or the other question, invading my personal space, - those are easily deflected. Only a few extroverts can resist outstanding compliments. This sounds a trifle mean, I know, but somehow one needs to protect oneself so as not to slide into a social burnout.

What comes up in small talk a lot are *trends*. I detest trends, but even more, I dislike it when others comment on the subject. To dictate trends is just another way of imposing external control. The industry tries to determine everything: how we have to dress, the colours we are allowed to wear this year, what kind of music is hip, which car we should drive and, of course, what to eat, read and believe. Aside from control and manipulation, they just want our money. No one thinks about the consequences for our environment either.

One day, my early aversion to trends must have turned into hate. To be honest, some fashion trends are simply annoying. The colours I prefer are not a matter of trends or fashion, but part of my nature, and therefore not easily to be changed. So, I get furious when someone tries to sell me things I don't like. As for cars, I don't even own one and don't care about them. It is crazy how much money people spend on cars.

I don't want to follow any trends, nor do I need them. I just do what feels right. Deep inside me, there is a sort of compass that guides me perfectly. It is my gut feeling and intuition, my sixth sense, and my sanity. Meanwhile, I have made it a habit to listen to each. If I don't, I end up like *Little Red Riding Hood* in the forest. I have learned it the hard way, more than once.

What about *parties*? When I turned 16, everyone else from my class was allowed to attend public parties until midnight, save me. I needed to be back home by 10 p.m., which was ridiculous since every decent party did not start before that time. So, I was petulant and stayed home on Saturday nights. I did not want to embarrass myself in front of my classmates. After a while, my parents interrogated me why I would not go out like other girls of my age. Having learned about my reasons, they allowed me to stay longer, but still, I needed to be home by midnight.

Fine, I went to a few parties. However, the best part was the time before the party when my friend and I dressed up for the evening. Of course, we had lovely talks and not just about boys. But to tell the truth, I found parties tiresome. Some of the older guys' behaviour was disgusting and disrespectful, and lots of them got drunk. Thank God, there were no drugs involved because, in my hometown in East-Germany, there were none available.

It did not help matters that I was rarely asked for a dance. This could have been due to my lack of decent dressing for the occasion. I don't know. Or maybe the boys found me intimidating because I looked more like a tomboy. For a long time, I wasn't interested in becoming a woman at all, and was very frustrated when my breasts began to grow, ugh! That's when it hit me. Obviously, there was no escaping becoming a woman. In the end, I enjoyed being one, though.

Honestly, I could not understand why anyone would want to attend such parties. Where was the fun in that? Standing around with a glass of alcohol that smelled and tasted awful was repelling enough, but decent talk was impossible. Then, there was that deafening kerfuffle from the loudspeakers. What was I doing here? I loved music, but I really hated any kind of excessive noise and still do. When I lay in my bed after such disastrous evenings, my head spun like a wheel. I felt entirely out of place, out of joint and out of everything. Eventually, I gave up attending parties, although it did not help to get a boyfriend, but I could wait. I was a late bloomer anyway.

## Burnouts

Despite mainly talking about introverts, I am sure that at some point, socializing is draining for everyone. Introverts might reach higher levels of fatigue during and after socializing, though. Lots of factors affect the outcome, like the intensity of interaction and how many people we meet.

Before I read *Jenn Granneman's* articles about introversion, I was not aware that we can end up with an *Introvert Hangover* or *Burnout* after too much socialising. So, I carefully studied the points she made and was astonished about the result regarding myself. On her website, Jenn pointed out different signs of an *Introvert Hangover,* for example:

- *"Every little thing is getting on your nerves.*
- *You can't think clearly.*
- *You're tired.*
- *You feel depressed.*
- *You're not acting like your normal self.*
- *You just can't do polite chitchat anymore.*
- *You have an intense desire to be alone."*

(Jenn Granneman. August 11, 2018. 12 Signs You Have an 'Introvert Hangover' (Yes, It's Real). Retrieved from https://introvertdear.com/news/introvert-hangover-signs)

I understand that too much socializing can overstimulate us, for we don't get high off socializing as extroverts do, so we sort of shut down as a form of protection. Initially, I could not think of a moment when I felt like that and was inclined to dismiss it as something that luckily does not apply to me. How wrong! There *was* a time in my life when I experienced burnouts, three of them, for that matter. I just never linked them to socializing. Instead, I had put them off as a mere result of physical exhaustion. I was so blind!

My first burnout in 1996 lasted for 10 weeks, the second one in 2002 for about 4 months, and the latest burnout in 2010 raged on for nearly four years. All in all, it took me three full-fledged break-downs to wake up, to understand and to finally *act*, instead of keeping on *re*acting.

All this is true. During my third burnout, I experienced every one of the described signs in a frightening intensity. Back then, I worked as an IT Project Manager. In some ways, it was the perfect job for me, since I had all the skills and immense willpower to survive it for six years. Yes, there is a 'but' coming on. Only few people outlast this kind of job for more than a few years, and there is a reason for it. To manage external projects with customers meant I had to be on the road for at least four days a week. In my case, I used public transport. We project managers rarely saw our colleagues and spent the occasional day in the home office, if possible.

Although I have a driver-license, I never owned a car. Getting the license was just a test for me. It cost me dearly since I never used it. From my earliest childhood on, I knew that I don't want to drive a car, ever. I never found out where my aversion came from. Finally, I decided to just give it a try. The technicalities of driving and theoretical tests have never been my problem, so I breezed through them. What was my problem, then? Whenever I started the engine, the car came alive like a dangerous animal. I sensed a strange essence being at work, lurking in the dark under the bonnet. My whole body started humming, and every cell felt like it was splitting into a thousand pieces. My spirit began to reel. I also became aware of what could happen. If I'd make the smallest mistake, people could die. It was like one of these forewarnings I had in the past. By the way, all of them had come true. There was just one thing to do, and the decision was a piece of cake. An enormous weight slid off my mind. After passing the final test, I knew that I would never drive a car anymore, and it felt right.

Because of the professionally organised public transport in Germany, there is no problem to travel without a car. Still, some of my colleagues smirked at me as if something was wrong with me. In my opinion, it was much smarter to use trains. While the others were busy steering their cars, I sat comfortably in a train, dealing with emails, preparing for the next appointment, cat napping or listening to music. The same applied to the time after business hours. As this job went, we often used to travel from one city to the next. Sometimes, I arrived short of midnight in a hotel. How was one supposed to get enough rest with such a schedule?

The repercussions of this rat race are countless. For example, there is no time to nurture your friendships or to do anything private in the evenings. It is just about work, work and work. At the weekends, one was glad to get the laundry done and to see one's family, if at all. There was no time for hobbies or other harmless amusements, much less for friends or sports. On the trains, in meetings and in hotels, I was invariably surrounded by strangers. There was no chance at all for the tiniest bit of solitude. After a while, the first of the mentioned burnout signs started to show.

The worst thing was that at bedtime, I could not shut down anymore, and panic-attacks frightened me to death. I could not breathe, nor could I sleep. It was horrible. Who knew anything about socializing hangovers back then? It would have helped.

The question is why I did not do anything about it, but went on, pushing myself further for another three years? There are many answers to that. I remember having analysed my situation carefully and even came to the right conclusions. But there was fear of not being able to find another job at my age. Also, I liked what I did, and I was good at it. A big part of my refusing to see the truth must have been pride. I did not want to admit that I was not shaped for this kind of job, even though I had so many skills and was successful.

What got me thinking was realizing that I had run into the last stage of a distinctive depression. For quite some time, I had wondered why any kind of vitality had vanished from my being. I was feeling apathetic and depleted all day long. Even during my holidays, I could not bring myself to smile or to delight in hobbies. I had totally run out of steam. My friendships did not seem to have meaning anymore, either. The worst thing was that not even my beautiful, gentle daughter could shake me out of my pitiful state. I was wasting away in a pit, unable to crawl out or to take the helping hands reaching down to me. Nothing mattered anymore.

Being deep down in the dumps, I started thinking about how to end my life. There seemed to be only one way out of my misery. Don't laugh at me, but I seriously went through any kind of possibility to kill myself. To hang myself was out of the question, although I could have followed my grandfather's example here. He had hanged himself in a shed when my father was 12 years old, so I never had the pleasure to meet my granddad. Ok, this was not for me, because I feared that it would not work.

So, poison then? As it turned out, it was not that easy to poison myself either. Aside from the fact that I could not get my hands on the necessary ingredients, I could end up an addle-brained survivor. Not a good option. The same could be said for jumping from a bridge or in front of a train, for other people could possibly die too. Then, there was this tall white tower across from my window. I could try that.

While still musing about self-deliverance options, I began to imagine myself dead. One day, I tried to change my point of view to that of my daughter. What I experienced in her spirit changed everything. How could I be so selfish and stupid? Had I forgotten about the difficult, yet happy time of my pregnancy? Or when I held my lovely baby in my arms for the first time? What was I thinking to leave her alone in this cold world? She needed me because I was her mother. If I killed myself, my daughter would always feel guilty for not having been able to save me. *"Why didn't you talk with me?"* she would have asked over and over.

What about my late mother? She was watching over me, of this I was sure. Although my mother had already passed away by that time, we were still connected. How could I throw away everything she had done for me? Could I really neglect her love and all she had taught me? My mother was the sweetest and strongest person ever. All I ever wanted was to be like her. Maybe it was about time to straighten my back to get out of that pit, - leaving self-pity behind. Suddenly, I knew the way and what I needed to do.

After weeks of detailed self-reflection and analysing, I decided to take a planned timeout. When I spoke to my doctor, he warned me not to prolong my torment any further. I didn't. First, I finished all my projects so that other colleagues could take over in my absence. At the beginning of spring, on the first of April, I said to my doctor: "*Here I am. Let's get started. I know exactly what to do and how to cure myself, and I don't want any pills.*" He gave me a sick-leave for the first two months and trusted me to do the right thing. He is a remarkable doctor, one of '*the old school*'.

During the following 7 months, I let spirit and body rule my days. For about 3 months, I slept 14 hours a day until exhaustion slowly began to level out. I made no appointments but lived in and for the moment. In the mornings, I played the harp. After enjoying my freshly cooked lunchtime meals, I went to the woods for walks or did cycling. Breathing in nature as deeply as I could, I paid attention to the small things out there. All the humming, the light, the tweeting, the rustling, and the awakening spring were balm to my senses. My smile returned, and I felt great. There was no room for thoughts about business or negativity. My world had become bright again, and I felt calmer than ever.

After a while, I developed an inexplicable faith in my destiny and that it would provide me with anything I needed. It was just a matter of trust and letting go of too much control. We humans rarely know what is good for us, until we really understand what life is about.

What can I say? It worked. After 5 months, my depleted well had been fully refilled, but I still wanted to build up a reserve, so I stayed home for another 8 weeks. Then, I was ready to look for another job, and I found exactly the one I had wished for. Finally, I had truly learned my lesson. Having turned over a new leaf, I never had socializing burnouts again.

Often, I went astray in life, but every time I fought my way back, and that is what matters. There is no way I am going off the rails any-more. Sometimes, I think back to the black chapters of my life. Yet, I don't dwell on my faults, but on the lessons learned and how I weathered the storms.

Vividly, I remember another story from vis-iting a public party. About 20 years ago, one of my former colleagues had become a mother. Being a sucker for babies, I visited her, she lived near Stuttgart. If I recall correctly, the baby refused to breastfeed and did not seem to be comfortable most of the time. When I held her in my arms, I had the impression of a high-ly sensitive and intelligent being looking at me.

Her mother was an extrovert and did not seem to pay too much attention to the baby's needs. She put herself first, which was selfish.

At that time, the *Cannstatter Wasen* was in full swing, a party much like the *Oktoberfest* in Munich. I could not believe it when my former colleague announced she would be attending the big party. To my utter dismay, she wanted to take the baby with her! I tried to convince my colleague to leave her daughter at home in my care because certainly, such a party is no place for a baby. Secretly, I had hoped to escape the party too. Alas, she would neither budge nor listen to me or her husband, so we went to the *Cannstatter Wasen* in the evening, the baby's normal bedtime.

The first thing that annoyed me was the ear-splitting noise coming from everywhere. There was no escaping from it. If one made the mistake to talk to someone, a sore throat was inevitable the next day. The crowd in huge beer tents and outside made it nearly impossible to move around. Some people's behaviour reminded me of animals rather than human beings. The brazen prices for food, which could only be called robbery, left me speechless. Unfortunately, I despise the music that is played everywhere at these kinds of parties in Germany. Nonetheless, most people enjoyed themselves considerably. For me, it was one of the most horrible experiences ever.

As for the baby, it had fallen asleep in the pram on our way to the party. As soon as we arrived there, the little girl started wailing, obviously protesting rightly against the onslaught on her senses. She would not stop, no matter what we tried. Finally, I enwrapped the baby in my coat, cradling her close to my body and walked about, trying to find a quiet corner, which was difficult. At some point, the baby fell asleep for an hour, until the mother insisted on taking her back. Of course, the wailing started again. The worst thing was that I could feel the child's pain as vividly as my own. It was almost unbearable.

Yet, the mother did not learn anything from the evening. I never saw her and her family again. It took me a long time to recover from this party. Until today, I do not understand why sensible people would want to attend such events, much less taking a baby with them.

## Extroverts' Hell

Here comes a story about someone who obviously detests solitude. As to be expected, most of the colleagues in my team are extroverts. Recently, I had an interesting conversation about the matter of introversion versus loneliness. Seated right beside me in the office there is a young man who is married and a father of two children. Soon, I discovered that he is a distinct macho-type and considers himself infallible. He hates any kind of criticism of his person and quickly gets angry. Also, he dislikes it when someone gives him good advice. On the other hand, he is full of good ideas and always willing to help others.

Anyway, one day he came to the office, having caught a major cold. Sneezing, sniffling and coughing, he sat beside me, generously sharing his germs with the whole team. The ungrateful bitch that I was, I asked him very politely if he would mind going to see the doctor instead of infecting everyone. Obviously, he did not get the message, for a wise and responsible person would not even have come to the office in the first place. He rejected my points in playing the hero: "*Ah, I am not that ill.*

*You see, I am still fit for work."* Translated, it meant: *Woman, - what are you talking about? Are you out of your mind? Don't get your knickers in a twist. I am a MAN. I don't get ill. Besides, what do I care about others' health?*

Well, the outcome for him was that he, of course, did not go to see the doctor. Thus, he did not get rid of the cold for about 4 weeks either. Ironically, I was the 'lucky' one, for a few days later I got ill and needed to stay home for 3 weeks. Due to a policy of our company, this also 'earned' me a personnel talk with my team leader. Great! They should have discussed the reason for my 15 days of sick-leave with the perpetrator, not with me!

Back in the office, I asked my colleague why he had not cured his cold at home. His laconic response was: *"No way! I get bored at home. I don't know what to do with myself."* What can you say to that? Staying at home alone obviously turns out to be extrovert's hell. The other downside is that when old and frail, such people have a problem keeping themselves busy. Often, they have no access to their inner world and are used to receiving stimulation only from the outside world.

My father, who died at the age of 94, was a typical example of this. During his last 4 years, he was convinced that a slow, painful death awaited him. Thinking back, I guess, he had by then developed a depression. All his children lived abroad, and despite the distance of 600 kilometres, I visited him once a month. His best friends paid him a visit nearly every day. Yet he became more and more dissatisfied and unwilling to entertain himself.

Mind you, he was a physically healthy man until the end, living in a flat where care was provided, if necessary. My father could still walk although he preferred to drive a car, which was out of the question at his age. Unsuccessfully, I tried to encourage him to spend his days in activities he once liked or develop new ones.

One day, he asked me what other people do all day when they are alone. "*Well.*" I said, "*They do all those things you refuse to do, such as reading, watching TV, listening to music, going for a walk, playing a variety of games with their neighbours and so on.*" As for the latter, he was quite picky with his acquaintances, sometimes looking down his nose on people with lesser education, which did not help the matter. In the end, he died a confused, unhappy man who consciously refused to cope with the disadvantages of ageing and extroversion. It is one thing when your own mind starts clouding, but an entirely different one to observe this in your loved ones. First, there was just a sensation of helplessness in me. Later, the growing realisation followed that this can happen to me as well.

Whereas my father did a lot of complaining about his boredom, my mother never behaved as such. She was content in her own world, be it pottering about in the garden, cooking or reading for hours. She also liked sewing and to watch fantasy series on the telly. Never a word of complaint passed her lips. Neither did she give the impression of being unhappy. She must have been in incredible pain during the months before she died of liver cancer, but she did not let on. I am sure she had some inkling of her illness, but she hated hospitals and did not want to die in one. Alas, unfortunately, her wish did not come true.

# Advantages of Introversion

Regularly forced to alternate between being alone and being with people, introverts need to withdraw from the noise of the world every day for a few hours. What with being parents or/and having a fulltime job, it is a challenge to find these oases. To carve them out of a tight schedule is a strenuous effort at times, but if, and when we manage, there is a whole *prism of solitude* we can harness. Its luminous colours come in endless shades and varieties.

## Prism of Solitude

According to my understanding, the purpose of solitude is being alone and free of the presence of other people. Then, we don't bother with what other people do or find appropriate. Some introverts are not just looking forward to the solitude, but crave it like a baby the mother's milk.

In an article by the author *Amy Morin*, I have read that "*solitude is an essential component to our well-being and health and that building more solitude into our daily life might actually reduce feelings of loneliness."*

(Ami Morin. "n.d.". 5 Ways Solitude Can Make You More Successful, Backed By Science. Retrieved from: https://www.inc.com/amy-morin/5-ways-solitude-can-make-you-more-successful-backed-by-science.html)

There you go. The word *loneliness* was bound to come up at a certain point. In the same article, Amy Morin writes: *"Being alone and feeling lonely are two completely different things, however. Many people feel lonely even when they're in a crowded room. And some people spend lots of time alone without ever actually feeling lonely."*

That is exactly how I experience the latter state. In public, I often feel like a bird with clipped wings. It changes the moment I am alone, and it does not mean that I feel lonely. In fact, I only feel lonely when I am either surrounded by people I don't like or in a relationship with a person who does not understand my personality.

In her above mentioned article, *Amy Morin* also comments on the following topics regarding solitude:

- *"Solitude helps you get to know yourself.*

- *Alone time could improve your relationships.*
- *Solitude boosts creativity and productivity.*
- *Solitude improves psychological well-being.*
- *Being alone gives you an opportunity to plan your life."*

It sounds so easy and made me wonder why many introverts tend to forego personal space for the well-being of a group. Partly, it might be good-naturedness, but we also feel that we need to explain our actions, which leads to misunderstandings and rejection at the worst. My daughter and I stopped this nonsense long ago. By simply saying nothing we no longer defend ourselves.

How, when, and where we spend our spare time is none of other people's business. It is interesting how well it works, as soon as you take a stand and draw a line. Only a few are foolish enough to overstep it. Never provoke a *Leo*. My daughter and I both share not just the star-sign of the Leo but have been born on the Assumption Day.

Without solitude, I would never be able to get *to know myself*, that's true. The same goes for *creativity*. The best writing time is when I am utterly alone. Then, I can't even stand music. I prefer absolute stillness, although I am also known for once having written poems in bustling places. In stillness, my mind becomes clear and the thoughts begin to rearrange themselves in a most harmonious way. For me, this is a definitive sign of *psychological well-being*.

*Productivity* is a different matter. In any case, I prefer to work in a single room in the office, but I have also cultivated the ability to tune out everything around me if I need to concentrate on something. In my time as a project manager, I needed to hone that skill. Otherwise, I would not have been able to work on trains. Interestingly, I can perfectly write in crowded trains, where I feel like I am in a bubble. People tend to leave you alone when they see you are writing.

It is similar when it comes to planning my life. For that, solitude is optimal, but not necessarily so. Like my mother and my daughter, I am quite the *planner*. It comes in handy since we like to let our heads save our heels, and we rarely act off-the-cuff. It seems as if our brains are always on alert to plan something. No input from inside or outside escapes our astute cockpit up there. Everything needs to be sorted immediately or put into a mental waiting loop. This sounds funny but is rather hard work for the brain. A good plan is half the success for communication or handling tasks. Thus, we are ready for any kind of situation and challenge.

Is there anyone who likes domestic chores? I never met such a person, neither am I of this kind. That is why I plan all of them to be done during the week. Housework and shopping at the weekend are forbidden, even if I fail to finish the chores until Friday. Housework can wait. My apartment is very clean, and we don't want to overdo it, do we?

We introverts are known to be good at prioritizing our daily schedules and any kind of work, even in private matters. This way, mismanaging can be avoided. One must be really good and quite realistic to handle many things at the same time. Whereas my mother and I are naturals, my daughter prefers to take one step at a time.

Then, there is the challenge of travelling the world. For the time before and after a journey,

I feel an urgent need to plan big enough buffers. Otherwise, I get stressed. For me, good planning also requires a particular flexibility. On holiday I'm not interested in ticking off as many sights as possible. Instead, it is essential to adjust plans when the weather is not so good. Funny things can happen then...

Quite vividly, I remember a trip to Ireland with my friend H. It was a rainy day, which is why we had decided to stay in the hotel. Sitting on my bed, cosily wrapped in the duvet, I got caught up in a sort of writing frenzy. In tune with the pitter-patter of the rain, my friend was snoring peacefully on the other bed. I was engrossed in writing a scene about life and death when suddenly, the fire alarm went off. I thought I might die of a heart attack, and H. nearly fell out of bed. When I stuck my head out of the room, one of the room maids told me not to worry. It was just one of the regular checks. Right...

## The Sound of Silence

Silence is not always what it seems to be. Not for the first time, I ask myself if there is such a thing as pure silence. If so, I am not sure, I want to experience that. Yet, we introverted beings greatly appreciate what we call silence. I am a morning bird, so when everyone is still abed, I am more myself than at any other time. A similar feeling I have in summer evenings when the city slows down before sunset, although I rarely experience this. That is when I feel completely at ease.

My daughter says that there are times when she really can't hear a single sound, not the noise of the street, the twittering of birds or any electrical device humming. For her, these are moments of perfect peace. Then, she closes her eyes and enjoys how all physical and mental tension drains away. Alas, such moments usually are short-lived.

One day, when I started working in the office by 6 in the morning, I suddenly became aware of an unusual silence around me. For a while, I just sat there, listening intensely. To my astonishment, I discovered that it was not silent at all. Somehow, I had mistaken the absence of voices for silence. For example, I heard the buzzing of a lamp and the distant humming of refrigerators. Also, I became aware of overtones in the vast open-plan-office.

The first time I came across overtones and produced them myself was during a seminar of my qualification as a *Sound Therapist*. I am not sure if such a profession exists in other countries. Or, maybe, it has a different name. At that time, I was a qualified healer already. In my private time, I treated friends with universal energy, Jin Shin Jyutsu, massages, and other healing techniques. Then, I discovered the new world of *Healing Sounds*. This is something completely different from music as we know it. It is amazing what can be healed by sound and its effects alone. For example, one can combine singing bowls, overtones, monochords, and didgeridoo. There is such a variety to choose from.

Other instruments complete the range, such as wind chimes, gongs, ocean-drums and tuning forks. *Roland Hutner* was my teacher, and he taught us that the world is sound: *Nada Prana*. As soon as you think about it, everything becomes clear. Churches and even our bodies are resonating entities. Isn't that marvellous? After the seminars, one is a changed person. Every tone or tune suddenly sounds different, even the silence, which you discover has never been devoid of sound at all. Wow!

But there are sounds that I find very disturbing. It is what I call *noisiness*. It comes in the shape of cars, motorbikes, chainsaws and mowers, banging doors and dripping pipes, hammering and loud chitter-chatter. It is not just that it all feels like an intrusion. There is more to that. It makes me sick and aggressive too. Then, I wish I could live in a cave by the sea, where the tunes of waves would drown out everything else, filling my essence with sounds of healing energy.

Talking about the most pleasant sounds of nature... When I go hiking, I like to lose myself completely in the sounds of the forest. Near a winding footpath, there is one particular spruce, my favourite tree. It is standing tall and has strong visible roots, creating little caves above the ground for the Irish moss. Every so often, I lean on the tree trunk and look upwards.

## The Vale of Silence

*We decide*

*What we do and feel*

*Despair or hope, adoration or hate*

*In our hearts the Love remains forever*

*Where there is darkness, there is light, they say*

*And they are right, but we need to go a different way*

*Did you forget the treasure chest, built for stormy times?*

*The Vale of Silence is just a mirage, where words fill*

*The void of transient absence*

ISIS (2017)

Two things happen in these moments. While I watch the gentle swaying of the surrounding treetop canopies, I feel uplifted and weightless. Closing my eyes to savour the magic moment, I become aware of the intense buzzing of insects around me. Now and then, they are predominated by tweeting of birds, and I try to differentiate between the species. It is the sweetest music to my ears.

This state of total happiness is comparable with the moment after I have climbed a mountain and arrive at the Summit Cross. Looking around, being on top of the world and level with other mountain peaks, I realize that all my sorrows lie far behind me. Provided there are no other people around. No wonder that in these moments, I am not inclined to return to the madding crowd.

Have you ever listened to the birds' concert in the early morning? About an hour before sunrise, they gather on the roofs of the city. One bird begins, but little by little the throng joins in. Ethereal sounds swell until they join in a heavenly concert of inimitable tones of perfection. This is the voice of nature in its truest and purest appearance. There is no trace of disharmony, which is extraordinary given the sheer number of 'musicians' without a conductor. The variety of their sound sequences never ceases to amaze me. In these magical moments, the world seems to hold its breath, and I don't want this to end.

I am one of the creatures with heightened senses. It is curse and blessing alike. Usually, I cannot fall asleep without using earplugs. In particular, ticking clocks are nerve-racking. Then, I've got a problem with the absence of darkness in my bedroom. Any kind of LED light needs to be covered because it bothers me. This proves to be difficult in hotel rooms when I don't have tape with me. My body seems to fall asleep and to awake in accord with the sun. Since I started using earplugs and blindfolds, the quality of my sleep has improved considerably. I have heard people saying that they cannot fall asleep when it is too quiet. For me, it is exactly the opposite. There's an apt saying for that. *"One man's meat is another man's poison."*

## Silence is Golden

*There are a thousand*
*And one things*
*I want to say to you*

*Yet, I know the moment*
*You are before me*
*I won't be able to*
*Utter a single one*

*But somehow you will know*
*Somehow you will understand*
*Maybe the silence will convey*
*More than I could ever say*

OSIRIS (2016)

## The perfect Thinking Time

Being alone also means living in my head more than usual. It is a fact that I do my best thinking when I am alone. Writing this book is a good example. Without the still raging pandemic, it would be much more complicated to get on with the writing. For months, we were forced to stay home and to go out only when absolutely necessary. This was Heaven for me, though it might sound strange. At home, I can be as introverted as I want. Then, I am in my element. There is a remarkable quote by Albert Einstein and he was so right! I have experienced much the same: *"The monotony and solitude of a quiet life stimulates the creative mind."*

(Albert Einstein "n.d.". Goodreads. Quotable Quotes. Retrieved from: https://www.goodreads.com/quotes/ 1196663-the-monotony-and-solitude-of-a-quiet-life-stimulates-the)

It is not easy to describe how free I feel and how productive I am right now. Creativity bubbles in my head like fizzing sherbet. If not for the pandemic and its negative effects, I wish it would go on forever. The words come to me like worshippers to a Goddess, no kidding! In the beginning, my thoughts flow gently like rivulets, but then turn into torrents that need to be channelled to avoid buffer over-flows. At the same time, my spirit is totally at rest, confident, and comfortable. That is the perfect thinking time for me. Enfolding me like a tent of stars, the welcome silence is an unfailing source of inspiration and space where my thoughts and dreams have their home.

In the office, such a perfect state can rarely be accomplished. I am lucky to have mainly quiet colleagues in my cluster. But some of the buildings include open-space kitchens on each floor. Out of 9 hours, that place is occupied for at least 8 hours a day and many people chat too loudly. The groups also share the occasional video, where colleagues laugh like maniacs about the misfortune of others. Can you imagine working under such circumstances? It is unbearable.

Even worse than the noise is *what* they are chatting about. It regularly raises my hackles. Of course, we asked them to be quiet. We even consulted their boss and complained about it to the management. Nothing has changed. Also, we kept asking them to be quiet, but it was like banging one's head against a brick wall.

So, what else can an introvert do but cope? I do, but it burns more than half of my energy resources. Thinking is possible, but it comes at a cost.

Thinking often happens unplanned and subconsciously. Only when I am interrupted, I become aware of its consistency. Interestingly, most of the time, we are not *'thinking'* at all in a narrow sense. In fact, what our brain automatically does is associating. It compares new information with what is saved in our memory and comes up with solutions. This is what we deem the truth. But at times, our memory is unreliable, and over the years, memories change their details.

It was fascinating to discover that the more consciously I think, the better my decisions turn out to be. They are less emotional too. The process of real thinking is hard work, but I love it. It is very satisfying to get results that are not just mere reproductions of memories. Such achievements, performed by conscious thinking, may stem from creativity. When I experience such moments, they almost always happen in the tranquillity of solitude and silence.

My daughter definitely lives very much in her head. On the one hand she loves it, but on the other hand it is dangerous if thinking becomes brooding about unpleasant matters. Transcendental Meditation and positive affirmations help to break the vicious circle effectively. There are times when it is necessary to meditate more than once a day, because the sheer overwhelming flow of thoughts just won't stop.

My mother, I suppose, was glad for the ability to live in her head too. Like my daughter and I, she could imagine and dream what she never had in real life. It was the only refuge she could retreat to. Maybe that is why she kept reading fantasy novels until the end. Yet, I wish we had talked more about her inner life when we had the time. Now, I can only guess what made her truly happy or unhappy. My daughter and I have learned from the failures of my past. Every week, we meet for a 'Girls' Night', and talk about things that are important to us. There are tears of joy and sorrow, and we have learned that honesty is the best way to solve problems.

## A World of Details and Precision

To lose ourselves in a world of details is another similarity of our *'Spiritual Trinity'*. As highly sensitive women, we notice details that others might miss. For us, to be blessed with excellent observational skills is normal and we have never considered it special.

When I enter a room or a place, I start *counting* immediately, be it people, furniture, or other things. Once, I was forced to stand in a seemingly endless queue at the airport after the boarding had been announced. Slightly bored, I did not look down like most people, but upwards. That's when I discovered thousands of nails peeping out of the ceiling, pointing straight downwards. Excitedly, I began to count them and ended up with more than 18.000. Innocently, I asked a friend who travelled with me *"Did you know that more than 18.000 nails are breathing down your neck?"* Slightly taken aback he replied *"No. Where? How do you know?"* There you go...

Nowadays, everyone seems to rely on the weather forecast. It happens that it is accurate as well. We use the forecast too, but also have other advantages at our disposal. We observe the clouds, the weather vanes, and how the wind changes. Furthermore, our headaches are quite reliable. When my daughter suffers from them, the sun is to come back. When I am the unlucky one, we are in for rain and nasty weather. So, since we like to be prepared for changes in general, our heightened senses come in handy.

In the office, there is an air conditioning system, blasting cold air from the ceiling. Oddly, I am always the first who feels it. It is the same with sensing strange odours, wafting through the floors now and again. I can smell smoke long, long before others become aware of it.

Then, there are *colours*, which I am somewhat picky about. Believe it or not, I cannot stand to wear more than 2 or 3 different colours on my body at the same time. With my auburn hair, I must be careful. I always liked colours such as blue, particular shades of green, and yellow. Shades of black and white are my other favourites, although they are not real colours. I love colour variations in general, but do not approve of all of them. That is why I cannot bear the apparel of African people.

They wear any kind of colour in every possible combination. Strangely, I experience this as a kind of assault on my mental order. Would they understand? I don't know.

Another fascinating aspect of our world of *details* comes to mind. It is the one about *precision*. Whenever I demand correct expressions in speaking or writing, I get teased by extroverts because I prefer structure and precision. It also happens when I insist that my cups belong in a particular cupboard. That is why sometimes I am called a nit-picker. Maybe, this is part of my autistic tendencies, but in any case such details are essential for my mental well-being.

Musing about noticing *details*, it came to my attention that I am very good at seeing *patterns*. It is hard to explain, but obviously my brain scans everything meticulously and automatically. In doing so, it recognises the slightest pattern in things. After comparing the perpetual flow of information, it files them away instantly. It happens with the strangest of things or events. Sometimes, the results come up in the shape of ideas to sort out problems, which is very helpful in IT support matters. At other times, my engineering skills break through and provide me with concepts to fix or construct something. Very often, it surprises me, because I even see patterns regarding things I have not the slightest knowledge of.

Ah, yes. Of course, there is a story coming on. It is about music and its patterns. About 10 years ago, I embarked on learning to play the Celtic harp, which gave me much pleasure. When I put my mind to reach a goal, I won't rest until I have succeeded. So, I exercised nearly every day for about an hour. At first, there was an obstacle to overcome, though. I was not able to read music, never have been. To me, all the notes look alike, these stupid little black dots on the paper! Musicians assured me it would come to me eventually. Unfortunately, it did not.

So, what was to be done? To give up was out of the question. I just needed to find a way to circumvent the part in my brain that refused to cooperate. *Ha*, I thought, *if I can learn more than 100 poems by heart, I might as well be capable of memorizing music regardless of my inability to read notes fluently.* Indeed I was. Every new piece of music I wanted to play, I hammered into my memory. Step by step, painstakingly translating note by note, they went into my fingers, albeit in slow-motion. It took me weeks, sometimes months to learn a new tune. Isn't it unbelievable that after all these years I still cannot read sheet music?

Anyway, after the first few months of endless self-torture, I went to a seminar for harp beginners. All the other attendees could read music, so I was at a disadvantage. Plus, as an introvert, it sometimes takes a month of Sundays to learn things, so no walk in the park at all. One afternoon, our teacher put us to the test. *"I am going to play a piece that sounds very strange. It will be nearly impossible to pinpoint what underlying melody there is to it. I want you to listen carefully and then tell me which melody the tune is based on."* Well, I just sat back with folded arms and relaxed, for I was sure I wouldn't recognize it anyway. I was not a professional musician, couldn't even read music, so no chance. Of course, I listened as everyone else did, but our faces stayed blank. The melody did not seem to be recognizable indeed.

When no one provided an answer, I started laughing and blurted out somewhat sheepishly: *"I don't know what it was. The music has confused me. There was no real structure to it. But somehow, the bass line did sound like the song House of the Rising Sun."* Upon my remark, the teacher's face lit up, and he said: *"Precisely."* I did not know what to say. Everyone was staring at me in disbelief. So, there was a pattern to the tune after all, and I had recognized it. I am still stunned by the revelation and have no explanation.

## The Art of Concentration

I am not sure if concentrating for long periods on something that matters is an art, but it certainly is a virtue. In our family, introverts and extroverts alike possess it. Even my father, as an inherent extrovert, could concentrate for hours on things. Most of all, he loved gardening, sports, and exploring nature.

Our '*Spiritual Trinity*' has always loved extensive reading. Without moving a muscle, we can sit or lounge somewhere reading novels for ages. We don't get hungry, we don't get tired, and we are not aware of our surroundings. The same can be said about working in general. Whatever we work on, we can go on as long as it takes, no matter if it leads to physical or mental overload.

At the age of 18, I had a knack for creating *cut-outs*, although I cannot say where this came from. Today, I wonder how I managed to draw the barely visible patterns with a pencil on black paper. Of course, my eyesight was so much better back then. There is one cut-out I remember in particular. All in all, it took me 8 hours to draw it and to cut it out with my father's dissection scissors. All the while, I did not leave the chair. My mother asked me a few times if I did not want any food, but I declined. I am not even sure if I replied at all. I was so immersed in my crafting that the world had ceased to exist altogether, and it made me happy. Therefore, people think I am *patient*. In my opinion, I was never a patient person, mainly because of my choleric temper. Most times, I am indeed very patient with others, but with me and my own deficiencies, that is a different kettle of fish. While musing about patterns, I realized their harmonizing effect on my spirit, which is a nice side-benefit.

*Writing* is another example of concentrating on things I like. Take this book. I started writing it during my holidays. As a disciplined person, I did not write for more than 9 hours a day. I could have, but I learned my lesson well about the necessity of taking breaks in between. In the mornings, I wrote for about four hours, non-stop. After cooking and having lunch, another three hours followed before I indulged in a snooze. The late afternoons were reserved for the rest of my writing hours or sports.

Regarding troubleshooting, I am renowned for never giving up until I am successful. Whenever I have worked myself into one of my notorious research-frenzies, colleagues and friends call me lovingly a *bulldog*. They swear I am short of snarling if things don't turn out the way I want. It is funny how time ceases to exist then. There is just one goal: that is finding the fault and providing a solution. In such moments, I seem to shape-shift into a spiritual, bodiless entity. Seemingly, there are neither boundaries nor limits to anything. It is an utterly pleasant state of consciousness, which is hard to describe.

Also, I have been blessed with the talent to manage many *parallel projects simultaneously*. To call it *'multi-tasking'* may not be entirely accurate, because these moments are rare when we indeed perform different tasks at the same time. For instance, I can listen to music or chats on the radio while I am cooking or cleaning. However, it is quite tricky to think about different matters simultaneously. This is a real challenge, although it can happen when I learn poems by heart. While I recite one line, I am able to already visualize the next line in my mind, so as not to lose the connection.

When I talk about parallel projects, I mainly relate to IT projects and requests I am responsible for in my job. I don't have the privilege to just work on one project at a time. There are lots of loose ends to control, and every day, new challenges come my way.

Young people of the new generation possibly cannot imagine life before computers existed. I have lived this kind of life until I was 23 years old: no landline, no smartphone, no internet and no social media. There was the occasional written or typed letter in the office, but we used to work at a different pace. Today, there is such an overload of information. It is beyond me how we survive this. No wonder that so many people suffer from headaches, burnouts, and other illnesses.

## Pros and Cons of Self-Learning

Having been raised in a family of teachers, one should think that self-learning was not a topic at all. My mother, father, uncle, and my eldest sister could have taught me everything. Instead, my parents were advocates of a strict upbringing. Laziness or avoidance of learning did not stand a chance.

It is not that my parents refused to help us when we did not understand things. They just expected us to do our own research first. Whenever I asked about something, they pointed to the intimidating-looking bookshelf beside my father's desk. Always, they encouraged us to read up about the matter before we discussed it. As a child, I sometimes saw myself as a victim of their profession. Now I know better. In fact, I am very grateful for their insistence to partly teach myself. It turned out to be one of the keys to success.

The *joy of learning* was always an intrinsic part of me. It helped me in situations, when my parents have not been able to help, or if they did not have the time. When I turned 14, I discovered that my father had the habit of writing shorthand when scribbling notes. That fascinated me and I decided to teach myself. No sooner said than done. I purchased a set of books about shorthand and went to work. Every day, patiently, I learned my lessons. To keep in practice, I wrote my diary in shorthand, which was thrilling. One of its side-benefits was that nobody could read it, except my father, who would never have done such a thing. Besides, my father had told me that another person's stenography is hard to read.

Years later, when I started playing the harp, I took about eighteen lessons. After that, I continued teaching myself. Many a time, I had watched musicians playing. Thus, I knew that it was crucial to learn the proper technique of how to set and move one's fingers on the strings. That's why I insisted on doing simple repetitions of basic movements during the first three months. My teacher Manfred appreciated it. Nonetheless, he wondered why I was not interested in learning as fast as possible, but as perfectly as possible. His other pupils have been more interested in learning tune after tune instead of caring about their playing technique. After the first year, my patience had paid off when Manfred said: *"Of all my pupils, you not just have the best technique, but you are on a two years' level already."* His compliment has helped me enormously to go on.

My enthusiasm and determination to play the harp came from visiting medieval fairs. There, I had the pleasure to watch harp players, dressed up to fit the occasion. From the first moment on, I was enchanted by this gentle kind of music that seemed to be divine, as if God-inspired. Back at home, the spell was still intact. As a sanguine person through and through, having discovered something interesting, I went to work immediately, trying to find out everything about harps.

Years later, a similar thing happened when I watched *Poi players* perform *fire shows* at medieval fairs. This was not just about the fascinating light effects and the music. The self-learner in me observed the performers' techniques closely, so as if to figure out how they do it. It goes without saying that one cannot simply start playing with fire in the yard. A solution was provided by one of my best friends G., who I attend medieval fairs with. She had been inspired by *Poi players* too and came up with exciting alternatives, called *LED Poi*. More so, she had already trained herself and could teach me the first moves. The rest I learned from videos because a picture is worth a thousand words. The word *Poi* originates from New Zealand and means *ball*, although nowadays, other objects rather than balls are used too.

Of course, it is not as easy as it looks. As with everything one wants to learn, the first rule is not to give up. The body needs time to adjust to the unusual moves, especially when you begin to move the Poi and turn yourself simultaneously. It can be hard at times, but to get bent out of shape doesn't help the matter! After a few weeks of practising, it became one of my favoured ways to keep fit. Moving the poi in harmony with the music has something magical about it. In summer, it is a real pleasure to play outside, especially when it is dark. In winter, it can be a good sport alternative to be exercised at home. Aside from *LED Poi*, I also like to use scarfs, shawl-extensions and wings.

**Good Listeners**

I have heard people saying that we introverts are known as good listeners, but impatient sometimes. Well, we are not just listening carefully, but also do it without changing the subject and making it about us. As described before, my patience depends on certain conditions. When I listen to my friends, my patience has no boundaries. In business matters, though, I still need to learn to keep my mouth shut. Too often, I cut others short because I cannot wait to speak my mind, especially when I think they are wrong. A bad habit indeed! The more I like someone, the more likely I am to be a good listener, which could be deemed as picky (which I am guilty of). A bit more of the restrained type of introversion would do me good.

My mother and my daughter are so patient when it comes to listen to people and to express their opinions. I admire them for these virtues. Hopefully, they will rub off on me someday.

Thinking back to my times as a fulltime software supporter, it is strange that I never had such problems at all. For nearly 8 hours a day, I did listen to the customers carefully and patiently. Otherwise, I would not have been able to do a proper job. I got good marks from them too. It was a difficult task because most of the customers had major software problems. Not everyone was friendly and understanding when it took time to come up with a satisfactory solution. The more astonishing was my patience with them.

Sometimes, I think that for enjoying music, one does not need to be a good listener. But if you are, beautiful things can happen. When I listen to music, the notes begin to turn into pictures, and very often of graceful ballet dancers. I can see them before my inner eyes like in a movie. There are moments when classical or choral music makes me feel like kneeling down, swearing that from now on, I want to be good and pure of heart eternally.

That was when a friend who is a professional musician said to me: "*I wish I could hear music as you do.*" When I asked him about what he meant, he told me that professional musicians would have the tendency to analyse and dissect music to no end. Maybe it is different for me because I cannot read music. If that is true, then I am glad I lack this ability.

There is something else I like to listen to. It is the *wind*. Maybe, the wind's mystery lies in its appearance, for no one has ever *seen* the wind. It is a phenomenon because we only perceive things moved by air. But we never see the wind itself. Oh yes, - there is a variety of scientific explanations for how it comes about, where it comes from, and how strong it is, but the wind is *de facto* invisible. At times, it feels like the soft touch of an angel. I have yet to see one either...

Whatever the wind is, magical fingers are at play, I am sure. Have you ever heard Aeolian sounds? They are so ethereal and impossible to describe. Once, on a hot summer day, I went with my friend F. to a church, where just for fun I played the harp, accompanied by his flute. Afterwards, we went outside. The church was situated on a hill overlooking a beautiful landscape. While I sat quietly on a bench, suddenly a wind got up and went through the strings of my harp. That was the first time ever I heard Aeolian sounds. It was a breath-taking experience.

Even at home, under my dormer roof, the wind plays concerts with a whole orchestra. Especially on stormy nights, I like to listen to the celestial music before I fall asleep. Its varieties never cease to amaze me. Gentle tunes become lively sonatas, and after a while, they turn into passionate symphonies, gone with the wind.

In such nights and especially during the *12 Holy Nights*, it sounds as if the Wild Hunt is out and about. Then, I imagine Odin passing my house in fierce pursuit with his ghostly group of hunters. I have heard it was believed that during their sleep, people's spirits could be pulled away to join the convoy. What a disturbing thought! Then, some see the Wild Hunt as a possibility to an opening up of the senses. In a way, it is an initiation into the wild. Also, it is about the confrontation of death and fears. Legend has it that the Wild Hunt's real purpose was to re-establish the former harmony between nature and individuals. I think that this balance has been destroyed long ago when Goddesses have been replaced by male Gods.

When the wind stills after a storm, I imagine a throng of fairies dancing and frolicking above my roof. I never feel threatened, but imagine being one of them. On the contrary, I even feel closer to nature, being part of its soft breath. Becoming aware of such details is nearly impossible if someone else is with me. I cannot say where it comes from exactly, but even if the other person is asleep, it is not the same as if I am alone. Somehow, I only connect with nature and the spiritual world fully, when I am utterly alone.

There are times when I ask myself if we listen with our ears only. I don't think so. In moments of pure stillness, all my senses seem to listen to the world. It also happens during my sleep. While the consciousness is at rest, my spirit is working hard to digest the information overload of the past day. It is like transforming physical things into spiritual ones, so the spirit can grow and reach higher levels. I wish I had time to study all my senses more closely. So many fantastic insights are waiting to be brought to light. Yet, we are wasting so much time with unimportant and unnecessary things! Well, it is not yet over, is it?

## The inner Monologue

The inner monologue never stops. True. That applies to our *'Spiritual Trinity'* too. On her website, *Jenn* described the matter as such:

*"You have a distinct inner voice that's always running in the back of your mind. If people could hear the thoughts that ran through your head, they may, in turn, be surprised, amazed, and perhaps horrified. Whatever their reaction might be, your inner narrator is something that's hard to shut off. Sometimes you can't sleep at night because your mind is still going. Thoughts from your past haunt you. 'I can't believe I said that stupid thing … five years ago!'"*

(Jenn Granneman. August 13, 2018. Introvert, Dear. Retrieved from https://introvertdear.com/news/ introvert-undeniable-signs/)

I could not have put it better! There was one thing that helped me immensely to stop unwanted inner monologue. It was the learning and daily practising of *Transcendental Meditation* ™. I can't believe it had already started 20 years ago! At first, I was sceptical and could not imagine it would help me. It did not take long to internalise the procedure, but it was hard to come to terms with what happened during the sessions. Everyone got a personal mantra, and there were some general rules to follow. Back then, I suffered dearly from asthma and other health problems. There was no moment when I could breathe properly. The TM teachers told us that it could take months until there was any kind of improvement.

Well then, I was highly motivated, so I began with 3 meditations in absolute solitude every day. After a week or so, I noticed the first changes in my breathing, albeit during the sessions only. Those were amazing moments. As soon as I could stop that endless stream of thoughts in my mind, even for a few seconds, my breathing slowed down immediately, and hope began to blossom in my tortured soul. The meditation proved to be so effective that I stuck it out until today.

It is said that this sort of meditation cures everything which is out of balance in body, soul and spirit. My own story is confirmation of that. Gone are asthma, panic-attacks, the pain in my back, and what else haunted me in the past. There TM has other positive side-effects too. There are things you have forgotten about? Suddenly, you can remember or find solutions for problems. You want to make a wish come true or like to change your personality? Phrase it before you start meditating, and there is so much more.

As you surely have experienced yourselves, life is a constant up and down of more or less pleasant events. That is why we fall into the occasional abyss and need to find a way out until we have learned the lesson. Inevitably, the day came when all the meditations did not help any further and constantly nagging thoughts in my head made falling asleep nearly impossible.

One night, when it could not get any more frustrating, it happened. A blurred fragment escaped my memory and presented itself as a life-saving beacon in the dark. It was not a thought, but a mere picture. In my mind, I saw the ancient Greek scholar *Archimedes* stepping into his bathtub. After noticing that the water level was rising, he proclaimed his famous words: "*Eureka, Eureka!*" Suddenly, Archimedes realised that the more his body sinks into the water, the more water is displaced. That means where one entity is, there cannot be another at the same time.

Suddenly, I was wide awake: OK. What if this principle also applies to spiritual things like thoughts? Could it be possible, and if, how could it be done? The short TM mantra obviously did not always work wonders. Then, I remembered my childhood days, when we used to learn and recite poem after poem in school, and I loved it. On the spot, I decided to give it a try. The very next day, I started to learn the first poem by *Johann Wolfgang von Goethe* that came to mind. On and on it went, and I learned many poems by heart. You possibly guess it already. Since then, the repression of unpleasant thoughts worked perfectly.

So, every time, when unwelcome thoughts haunt me, I mentally begin to recite poems. During the process of learning, something else beautiful happens: with every repetition, another piece of the poem's meaning unravels. It is comparable to having an epiphany. Whenever I thought I knew what the poem's message was before memorizing it, I was mistaken. Only when I had it safely stored in my memory, the whole secret was revealed. The great feeling of having discovered something precious is unique. After practising for a while, I noticed another positive side-effect, aside from training my memory. These lyrics (especially the mysterious ones by *Rainer Maria Rilke*) always put me in a good mood and destroy every single negative thought. It is like fighting the darkness with the might of light.

As for dealing with negative or unpleasant thoughts, 15 years ago, I came across another helpful technique. It is directly associated with the keys to fulfil your wishes for success, wealth, and happiness described excellently in *Pierre Franckh's* book *The Desire Code*. The secret lies in using the right affirmations. True, there are days when the simple ones are not strong enough. That is why I have invented several affirmations to stop negative thoughts, such as: *"In my private time, I think personal and positive thoughts only."*

Most of the time, it works as intended. Aside from dissolving negative thoughts, it inhibits me from thinking about business matters when unsolved problems trouble my mind. It goes without saying that there are thoughts I do not want to shut up, for instance, when I am writing prose or poetry or when reflecting on things consciously.

My mother never did meditate, but my daughter does. In time, she also began working with affirmations, and successfully for that matter. You could say that meditation is an effective method to keep the inner monologue at bay. It is also regarded as a cure for many diseases without any negative side-effects. Given the advantages, it is surprising that this gentle healing method is not used more often.

## Writing versus Speaking

There is another statement that got me thinking: *"Introverts "often feel as if they express themselves better in writing than in conversation," writes Susan Cain in her revolutionary book, Quiet."*

(Jenn Granneman. August 15, 2019. The Science Behind Why Introverts Struggle to Put Their Thoughts Into Words. Retrieved from https://introvertdear.com/ news/the-science-behind-why-introverts-struggle-to-speak/)

Well, it applies to none of our *'Spiritual Trinity'*. Every one of us is as good at writing as at speaking. It must be the genes, then. Most of the time, my mother just never had the time to write, but when she did, wow! What talent! My daughter is very skilled too, but probably she would disagree, as she usually does when it comes to highlighting her talents. She might not feel the same urge to write like me, but she can write, believe me, and her imagination knows no boundaries.

As for preferring to make phone calls or writing emails rather than face-to-face meetings, my mother knew nothing of texting or emailing, and since she did not have a phone for most of her life, there were not many calls either. But in her later years, she enjoyed phone calls with her children, because all of us lived abroad.

As for my daughter and me, it depends on the situation as well as on the person. I meet my daughter once a week for a Girls' Night, whereas her mother-in-law prefers to text. With my friends, I prefer to use email, which is mutual. Nonetheless, when there is time, we love to talk on the phone for hours too.

People have asked me why I would not make a career out of writing or of my profession as a healer. I have thought about this very often myself. I even ran my own IT Company for four years. That is probably the reason why I don't want to do it. Working as a free-lancer taught me many things. There was always the underlying pressure of keeping the business flowing. I hated that. To be self-employed has the undeniable disadvantage that you cannot afford to be ill. Plus, as an employee, I am entitled to six weeks of holidays. Try that as a free-lancer, and you will see how difficult this can be. I did not want that either. It would be the same with writing or healing. Deep inside, I am an artist and want to be free to create what and when I want. Without any pressure, I prefer to set my own pace and to work on my own conditions.

By the way, I like this quotation, where *John Green*, author of the bestselling young adult novel, *The Fault in Our Stars*, says: *"Writing is something you do alone. It's a profession for introverts who want to tell you a story but don't want to make eye contact while doing it."*

(John Green. "n.d.". AZQuotes.com. Retrieved from AZQuotes.com Web site: https://www.azquotes.com/quote/599140)

It hits the nail on the head. I could not have put it better. Yes, writing definitely is one of my best strengths, although with a full-time job, it is hard to find niches to perform it. Also, my mind needs to be at ease and free of worries. I don't have difficulties writing technical documentation while being surrounded by people. But writing a book is different. That's when I really need to be alone and undisturbed.

Throughout the process of writing when one is less distracted by other things, it is much easier to produce coherent and profound thoughts. Whereas it is impossible to go back on rashly spoken words, you can delete written sentences without regrets. In a way, it feels safer than speaking. Letting your temper free rein in writing is not a disadvantage, but rather the opposite. Rewriting and editing follow later, and that is where solitude comes in handy too.

## Silence without You

*Dear Darling, - did you know*
*That silence once was full of words*
*As their shades carved sculptures*
*Of withered beauty in my soul?*

*Or have you heard that muted*
*Whispers cry sometimes aloud*
*When shards of pain rip slowly*
*Our wounded hearts in pieces?*

*Do you feel the time dissolve*
*Where spikes of silver shadows*
*Slide obliviously along the*
*Draught of trailing thoughts?*

*In my chosen solitude, I abide with*
*Your spirit's ageless presence*
*I have always loved the silence*
*But not a silence without you*

ISIS (2017)

## Curses and Blessings of Communication

The last century has provided us with a variety of hitherto unknown choices of communication. Many of us welcomed them without reservation because they seemed to extend our freedom considerably. Suddenly, one could make phone calls without being confined to a cable anymore. Years later, simple mobile phones became smartphones.

The invention of the internet opened unexpected windows for connections with a world of vast possibilities. Especially for introverts, this was a completely new channel *to communicate* and *not to communicate*, not to be seen, but to see and research in silence without the need to leave home at all. What a revolution! The downside for some people was that they felt lonelier than ever.

At some point, Apps have been invented, so we can talk while seeing each other's images via camera. On a large scale, letters have been replaced by emails, and social media groups sprang up like mushrooms. When the instant message services began to triumph, everyone seemed to be over the moon. The repercussions came later. With all these digital devices, people felt the need to be connected 24/7, not being aware that such activities wear them out in an entirely new dimension.

Once, I was having supper in an airport hotel. There, I watched an American family and was horrified by their careless behaviour. The parents paced back and forth between lobby and restaurant, making a fuss about nothing. Their about 10 month's old infant was wailing heartbreakingly. Overtired, the girl was rubbing her eyes with chubby fists. A blind person could see that the baby was exhausted and short of collapsing. Barely able to keep her eyes open, she stretched out her arms to be picked up by the mother or her grandmother, sitting beside the child.

Guess what they did? Instead of comforting the wee one, they placed a tablet in her hands, so she could play with Apps. While she pushed the computer away, the child's weeping increased, but the family just did not pay attention. The baby seemed to be like a piece of furniture to them. Three adults and none of them took care of the girl. They replaced themselves by a computer. What cruelty!

Another example of the downsides of 'Social Media & Co.' was one of the apprentices in my former company. He was an old soul, wise beyond his age and one of the most hyper-sensitive, introverted people I ever met. I liked the young man very much, and he was like a son to me. One day, we talked about the madness of modern technology, or rather the foolishness of people dealing with it. When I told him that I despise Facebook and WhatsApp & Co. and that I don't have any accounts there, he confessed to me that he had closed his accounts too. He could not stand the pressure, the mobbing, and the omnipresence of people in his private life. So, he simply shut them out. Brave decision!

Also, I find it necessary to control my mobile phone. First and foremost: it can be switched on and off, which some people seem to forget about. Then, I uninstall or at least deactivate any kind of App I don't want to run. The automatic location identification is only switched on when I need it. Almost all the time, I have my phone on mute mode. I do not allow myself to be bullied by a phone or any other technical device! The world is noisy enough without them. Often, when I have to explain my strict rules regarding mobile phones, I meet with incomprehension. People then argue that I might not get 'bad news' in time. This usually causes me to respond that 'bad news' still comes soon enough. Besides, this is none of other people's business how I deal with it. There are already enough other areas in my life where I have to endure a certain amount of external control, such as in my job.

As for 'bad news', about 25 years ago, I stopped reading newspapers, magazines and crime novels. The same goes for watching crime movies. They all had one thing in common: most of the information was negative, which amplified my breathing difficulties while reading. To my great delight, I discovered that life without this kind of literature or films is not just possible, but also much more enjoyable. Furthermore, there was another side-benefit. When you get right down to it, every kind of journalism seems to be designed to influence readers' opinions, and thus to control their behaviour. So, by avoiding the above mentioned subjects, I regained a freedom I had not missed until then.

## Times of enforced social Distancing

As mentioned before, I cope very well with the COVID 19 social distancing rules. The public health orders to stay put suit me just fine. Deep down, my life has changed for the better, because the alone time is rejuvenating. It is almost like an introvert's dream coming true. I don't have less to do than before, but more time to do things, which is relaxing in these times of capsule-living.

Right now, we introverts are at an advantage to cope with the pandemic situation. As individuals who not just don't mind being left on their own, but crave aloneness, we don't feel the urge to get together with people. Why would we be fighting regulations that give us so much more freedom and safety?

Naturally, some think that we introverts will eventually need to find ways to step up our own interactions with others. I don't think that applies to me or my daughter. For us, nothing has changed. With my friends, I stay in contact via email, phone or Skype, just like before. In addition, we revel in the unexpected newfound solitude and freedom to do things more uninterruptedly. Unfortunately, as an introverted person you have to justify yourself again and again for not seeking the company of other people. That can be quite tiring. So, in a way, the pandemic has provided us with a welcome excuse not to meet with anyone.

The outer world has become quiet, which gives us the chance using the time to enrich our lives in other ways than going out. Thus, introverts might fare better than extroverts at the requirement to stay away from others. I rarely go out for dinner anyway, so the restrictions do not bother me at all. I have always loved cooking. Isn't it funny that suddenly, extroverts find themselves living in our introverts' world since the social order has been turned upside down?

Where I live, we are still allowed to go out for shopping or for walks despite the general lockdown. On these occasions, I don't come across many people, and if, they dutifully keep their distance, wearing masks. In the beginning, most of us didn't wear masks until our politicians decided otherwise. It has been proven that masks don't protect you from getting infected by the COVID-19 virus. In fact, the masks give a false sense of security. People wearing them tend to get more careless. So, I stopped hunter-gathering in most of the nearby shops and switched to online shopping for a while, especially since in the meantime, some goods were in short supply. It worked just fine, although I'd rather support local business.

For me, the so-called *sacrifices* necessitated by social distancing are no sacrifices at all. Unlike extroverts, I don't need alternative means of interaction, such as video conferencing, during this time of social isolation. I just go on with my life almost as it was before. I couldn't meet my daughter or my friends for a while, alright. However, this is something we can deal with. We do not crave physical contacts, such as touch and handshaking, or the possibility of mirroring the behaviours of others.

Where extroverts feel energized by socializing, it is the opposite for me. My energy and power come from being isolated from others. In my secluded space, I just continue doing what I do best. Far from the madding crowd, I thoroughly revel in quiet days, safe in my 'castle' above the streets.

In the beginning, I felt a twinge of guilt, re-alising I might actually be enjoying the apoca-lypse. By now, I got rid of this ridiculous self-incrimination. The pandemic is not *my* doing, and isn't it a virtue to make the best of a diffi-cult situation? It is a 'Pandora's box', and I was not the one who opened it.

After the first two weeks of working in the home office, I noticed significant changes in my well-being. I feel much more rested after getting up in the morning. Even after eight hours of concentrated work at the computer, I do not feel drained at all, compared to work-ing in the office. I am quite sure that it has to do with the absence of other people and much less distraction.

Also, I get things done in a fraction of the usual time. It gives me pleasure to do things well. Working alone, I don't need to waste precious energy while holding up my mental shield all day long. I don't get pulled out of my work by untoward phone calls either. Aside from online meetings, everything is dealt with by email.

Another advantage comes to mind concern-ing my spare time. Usually, I need about one hour walking to the office and back. The home office option gives me the chance to get up later in the morning and to stop working earlier. It makes such a difference for how I can use my spare time! If not for the pandemic and its casualties, I wish it could go on like this.

There is something else. When I work in the kitchen, I used to listen to music from my playlists. Since the beginning of the enforced social isolation, I rarely do it anymore. I am so fascinated by the silence from outside and how it improves the balance of sounds inside that I just can't get enough of it. It is a great pleasure to listen to the sound of silence. Believe it or not, but I can feel its restorative effect immediately. In these moments, I seem to enter a whole new level of consciousness. It is not the music from outside I listen to any longer, but from my very essence, swinging in harmony with the sound of nature and stillness.

Extroverts, most likely will not experience the same because they possibly cannot stand silence for long. For them, it must be horrible to forego doing sports in groups, meeting each other or eating out. It seems that in this crisis, we are not all in the same boat. The clouds for them are silver linings for us. That's what I call temporary retributive justice.

The other day, I heard on the radio that introverted people start to feel exhausted because their calendars had filled up with *virtual happy hours*. To be honest, I did not understand the problem, because I regard this not as a matter of introversion, but poor planning and the bad habit of saying "*Yes*", when you mean "*No*". I mean, calendars don't magically fill themselves, do they? One can turn down an invitation. It can't be that difficult.

What also annoys me is some people's inability to adjust their lives for a few months for the sake of winning the fight against the virus and saving lives. Slowly, but surely, the whining about the necessary lockdowns and contact restrictions gets on my nerves. Not even in this precarious situation can they put their egos on the back-burner. I mean, really! There were times in history when there was much less comfort as we know it today.

Recently, I watched a film about The Middle Ages. This period is not that long ago and I asked myself what spoiled, pampered people would do if they were forced to live in ancient times. My guess is that they would last a day, - maybe two. People did not have hot water or water closets for that matter; - not to mention enough food, if there was any at all. Hmm, not to mention the thieves and raiders, although not much has changed since then aside from the laws, hasn't it? Well, at least I would have my sword and know how to use it. People slept on the ground then, and life was about surviving, not dawdling or squandering time and money. Also, I have my doubts about some modern people's capability for making fire. At least a toilet paper shortage would have been out of the question, for there was no such thing as toilet paper, ugh!

Meanwhile, we have reached a point where world-wide millions of people are infected with COVID 19 and many have died. Still, plenty of people demonstrate for easing the restrictions far too soon. They should take the example of a generation that suffered from The Second World War. These people know that it could be far worse than to remain in a lock-down in safe homes for months with enough food in their bellies and nothing to fear than their own boredom. There could be constant air raid warnings as well as bombs destroying families and homes. There could be famine instead of feast and unemployment instead of jobs. There could be war and apocalypse. If this quotation is not a fake, then Buddha had something to say about gratitude, which is still valid until today:

*"Let us rise up and be thankful, for if we didn't learn a lot today, at least we learned a little, and if we didn't learn a little, at least we didn't get sick, and if we got sick, at least we didn't die; so, let us all be thankful."*

(Gautama Buddha. "n.d.". Goodreads. Quotable Quotes. Retrieved from https://www.goodreads.com/ quotes/ 1655-let-us-rise-up-and-be-thankful-for-if-we)

## Sonnet

*O living will that shall endure*
*When all that seems shall suffer shock,*
*Rise in the spiritual rock,*
*Flow thro' our deeds and make them pure,*

*That we may lift from out of dust*
*A voice as unto Him that hears,*
*A cry above the conquer'd years*
*To one that with us works, and trust,*

*With faith that comes of self-control,*
*The truths that never can be proved*
*Until we close with all we loved,*
*And all we flow from, soul in soul.*

Alfred Lord Tennyson

Once, I have been accused of being egoistical by one of my acquaintances, because if necessary, I can set aside thoughts of a grieving world in the challenge of this unique situation of a pandemic. Yes, I am well and don't suffer at all. Gratefully, neither do my friends nor family. So far, I haven't lost any money or my job. Of course, the occasional question crosses my mind: will we enter a recession? Indeed, if we are not patient enough, more waves of the virus are most likely. The aftermath of this crisis for the world is not yet foreseeable. So many people have died or lost their jobs.

All this is true, but what good does it do me or others if I am grieving or let myself be consumed by fear about an unpredictable future? In my experience, people who just take pity on others cannot help. There needs to be a few who keep their cool. I'll cross that bridge when I come to it. Panicking has never helped. I am better at dealing with matters at hand, and as soon as they happen. I do not think this is selfish, nor is it a lack of compassion. It is a necessity for solving problems. Right now, I can help by sticking to the restrictions.

Now and then, I think about how we would have dealt with a pandemic forty years ago. Back then, I was in grammar school. We did not have smartphones, computers or the internet. Lessons could not have been taught online, and home office had not been possible either. Everything might have been much worse. I suppose, as a child, I would have surrounded myself with stacks of books and read until my eyes fell out of their sockets. Perhaps, people should think twice what they are complaining about nowadays.

In the meantime, more than a year after the pandemic started, the first vaccines are available and hope is blossoming. Yet, the first variants of the virus have already emerged, which complicates everything. I don't think that the worst of COVID 19 will be over before summer 2021. The vaccines may prevent us from dying, but it doesn't mean we can't spread it any longer. Let's hope, people get that and don't become careless.

I am still hesitant about forecasting people's behaviour after the pandemic. My guess is that many extroverts will return to excessive socialising as fast as possible, partying until they drop. On the other hand, we introverts will mourn the end of a too-short life in solitude. It will be hard to return to a world full of unnecessary noise. Most likely, we introverts will continue lingering quietly on the periphery of the madness surrounding us, while reading our books and bolting the doors.

## Myriads of Talents

It is said that introverts not only possess a wide range of interests, but myriads of talents too. It can take a while though to realize one's own skills. On a few of them, I have already reflected in this book.

After the Second World War, my mother became a teacher because it was her calling, and teachers were scarce then. Not only was she a fantastic tutor. Because of her love and dedication, she was good at everything she did. For me, she is the embodiment of love, burning brighter than the sun. I doubt that she knew about her many talents as a mother, teacher, wife and the exceptional person she was.

My daughter is very gifted likewise, but up to now, she refuses to acknowledge her virtues. To a certain extent, this could be my fault as a mother. For so many years, I have been a driven person and a perfectionist to the bone. It is possible that she felt unable to live up to parental expectations, even to the unspoken ones. As a single mother, I had to run a tight ship, after all. Unfortunately, I have not yet been successful in convincing her of her many talents. Hopefully, time will teach her about her own magnificence and beauty.

In another chapter, I mentioned the strict upbringing by my father. I suppose that this was part of the reason why it took me so long to discover, acknowledge and hone my skills. A few years ago, I visited my writer friend S. in Munich. After the fencing seminar, we sat together and discussed my doubts about being able to write a book. I said: *"What? I am just a normal person."* She protested instantly: *"Ha, you are the least normal person I know."* First, I was stunned by her response because I did not know what she was talking about. Then, she started pointing out some of my talents that until this moment, I had taken for granted.

On my way home, I mused about what she had said and surprisingly discovered more unexpected talents. She was right. Compared to many other people, my skills were exceptional, although I did not choose to keep my skills under wraps consciously. Since then, I saw myself and my virtues in a completely different light. Suddenly, I had found an explanation of why I could never choose a profession after leaving school. There were too many talents I did not even know about. Finally, it makes sense. Still, I am grateful to have studied industrial engineering and management. It combined two other talents of mine: a natural, scientific curiosity and an uncanny sense to analyse and manage everything, - anything. It even brought to light a skill I once refused to acknowledge I have: to master Information Technology.

Had I chosen differently, I might have become a brilliant lawyer, a creative architect, a passionate musician, and an encouraging consultant. Also, I could have turned into a resourceful interior designer, a patient psychologist, a skilled writer, a professional healer or even a wise philosopher. Maybe, because I had more than one string to my bow, I just could not decide.

In expressing this, I am reminded of The Sleeping Beauty, who had been blessed by 12 fairies. So, where is the catch, or rather the 13th Fairy in my case? If she had died already, the balance between good and evil would be out of balance. Thus, she must be hiding somewhere, or the 13th Fairy is possibly the one sleeping now. Who knows?

I am aware that it is hard work to develop one's own abilities and consciousness, but I have never been a coward or shied away from challenges. There is no fear in me to fail, be judged or ridiculed either. Except for my parents, my daughter and my friends, I never minded other people's opinion about me. My parents, God bless their souls, saw to that. There might be people who fear their own power, but I never did and never will. On the contrary, I am ready to explore the limits of my power. I wonder what happens if and when I reach them.

*Marianne Deborah Williamson*, American author, politician and spiritual leader, wrote: *"Our deepest fear is not that we are inadequate. Our deepest fear is that we are powerful beyond measure. It is our light, not our darkness that most frightens us. We ask ourselves, who am I to be brilliant, gorgeous, talented, fabulous?"*

(Marianne Deborah Williamson. "n.d.". A Return to Love: Reflections on the Principles of "A Course in Miracles". Retrieved from https://www.goodreads.com/ quotes/928-our-deepest-fear-is-not-that-we-are-inadequate-our)

Yes, indeed. That is the very question I ask myself since I began to think. It surfaced again when I achieved the first breakthrough regarding the healing sessions. I could not believe what people had experienced during and after my treatments. Could it be that I am *that* powerful? It can, and I am. There are still moments when doubts creep up my spine, but I have learned to silence them with positive affirmations.

Increasing field experience over the years helped me to stop hiding my light under a bushel. It was no easy task because I am well known for having brought to perfection ways of withholding my gifts from the extroverted world. I am sure that we are all meant to shine and to make a difference in our own ways. In fact, we introverts are real dark horses, standing out from the crowd unintentionally!

All my life, I had this feeling of being a '*dinosaur*' in a world where I don't belong. The same goes for my mother and daughter. We must have been left behind and forgotten during the Ice Age, maybe sleeping off centuries in a cave. The other thing is that I have this strange, but vivid consciousness of my past incarnations. When my feet first touched Scottish soil, I had the feeling of belonging and of coming home. It was the same in Ireland.

There are fragments of memory being a warrior. It fits, because even as a child I always felt like *Queen Maeve of Connacht*, semi-historical daughter of the great goddess *Mórrígan*, battling my way through life.

I remember clearly that as a child, I was not squeamish about what I wanted when I was with my chums. I wasn't known for going easy on others. They always gave me the evil eye when one of my feared tantrums was in full swing. I am not proud of that chapter in my life. Fortunately, I have grown out of temper tantrums by now. Well, almost... I am still a fierce warrior, but nowadays I am better at reining in my temper. Plus, I think before acting. There are still times when I wish to live in another chapter of history, but that is mere nostalgia. It is not that long ago when women did not have any rights. So, one should be careful what one wishes for.

Finally, I have embraced my talents and who I am, and I know that my spirit is immortal. I belong to myself and to the Universe. Thus, duality has vanished, and I have come home in myself, lastly. Writing this book has helped me immensely to clarify several aspects of my personality and to see things from different angles. It was like studying me through the eyes of another person. I am not longer afraid or ashamed of my talents. On the contrary, I have learned to acknowledge and enjoy my power. Furthermore, I became more willing and confident to explore its limits, and it feels good.

# Memories and Relationships

This chapter is about childhood memories, meditating on friendships in general and the relationship to my Twin Soul in particular.

## Memories

Reflection on introversion within my family brought me right back to my childhood days. My mother's brother R. lived just about a hundred yards down the road, and he was a textbook example of an introvert. My uncle was extremely shy and nervous, even among his family.

He and my mother had a delightful sense of humour, which made it such a pleasure to be in their company. In retrospect, I have the suspicion that my uncle used his humorous side as a shield to deflect the attention of others. He never spoke about himself. We loved him very much. His favourite game was chess, and he was a master player. Although he passed away 33 years ago, I can still visualize his dear face in my mind quite clearly.

Then, there was our nanny and her husband. They might not have aced at an IQ test, but they were very wise when it came to living an honest and decent life. They lived with her mother and two children in a little house with tiny rooms, like in a doll's house. All of them were introverts. They led a humble life with simple rules, no car, no fancy stuff and no surprises. To our delight, they raised rabbits in the backyard, and we used to provide them with potato peelings, which gave us the opportunity to stroke the rabbits' soft fur.

There is one especially vivid memory of my nanny E. and her husband W. sitting in the kitchen. There was a moment when they looked at each other with so much love that it was tangible. It was as if the world had come to a standstill, and only these two people existed. I have never seen anything like that shared love expressed again. For us children, E. was like a second mother. I have learned so much from her, still do.

Until the age of 92, she went for a daily two-hour walk, regardless of the weather. She was never ill or suffered from overweight. Until her death, she also kept her excellent hearing.

Three months before she passed away, attaining 99 years, we talked on the phone, and I was astonished, how clear-minded she still was. Somehow, her family never has been much afflicted with the general problem of introverts in an extroverted world. They just kept to themselves maintaining a low profile, which proved to be very healthy.

Back then, we lived in a town with about 80,000 inhabitants. Our family resided in a rented four-room flat in an apartment building with three entrances. All in all, there were 9 families and a few of them quite broken ones. Thinking back, it is astonishing that almost all those people were introverts to the core.

Everyone kept to themselves. It might also have been connected with the fact that all the adults worked fulltime. There is not much time for other things then. Spare time was practically non-existent. There were no parties, no noticeable neighbourly chats. It was as if everyone had something to hide (which they probably had).

It was different for us children, though, 13 altogether. Depending on age, we used to play loosely in little groups in the yard. Two of my playmates were very strange. The little boy was a mix of being shy and mean. His parents seemed to put a lot of pressure on him. They considered themselves superior to everyone else. The older girl seemed to be sort of crazy in a funny way. Years later, as adults, the girl and the boy committed suicide. In her case, it was especially hard, since she already had two children of her own. One day, she just jumped out of the window, and no one knew why.

But that's not the end of it. Unfortunately, there was another suicide in the neighbour-hood. The dentist, who lived with his wife in the apartment above us, had hanged himself. Well, at least he had a reason to do it. His spouse was a sinister and full-fledged witch, who could have rivalled Snow White's step-mother. One could see it in her eyes. Every cell of her screamed 'evil', whereas her fake smile and pretended friendliness deceived many people. Her negative aura contaminated the whole building, and I shivered whenever I passed her entrance door. Her late husband, though, was such a good-hearted soul, but unfortunately too weak to stand up to her.

In the past, things might have turned out differently, had parents known about introversion as we do now and treated their children accordingly. The question is if some people could have been saved by a different kind of upbringing. It is difficult to say, for the development of a person is influenced by so many other aspects too.

## Friendships

Somehow, I never had problems to make friends. The most successful tactic was to reveal myself quietly, but not to take the first step. All my friendships came to me this way with one exception, my friend G. We became acquainted through a medieval fair community. I contacted her first, and she responded. After the first meeting in my home, which was a bit awkward, we became best friends and now share quite a few hobbies.

With all my friends, I was able to forge lasting and meaningful connections, satisfying our limited need for social stimulation. Our quality time is intensive and inspiring. Together, we feel elevated and happy. We share so many interests, such as attending medieval fairs, fencing, Renaissance dancing, playing poi, writing, travelling and photography. Furthermore, we are interested in tarot cards, making music, reading, travelling, spiritual healing, gardening, cooking, and so much more.

The good thing in having introverted friends is that we don't need to talk about rules regarding solitude, socialising or intrusions. They go without saying. We also have no unreasonable expectations of each other. Beside all closeness, we stick to the rule *'A hedge between keeps friendship green.'*

Much has been written about the friendships in my life. We also established that nearly all my close friends are introverts. However, there was a time when I also had extroverted friends. In hindsight, I'd call them acquaintances rather than friends.

Admitting that once, I used one of these online dating services, is a wee bit embarrassing, but true. Like so many other people, I was under the misapprehension that it would be easier to find a fitting match there than in real life. Technically, this assumption is not that farfetched, because, in times of commuting between home and office and working fulltime, there are not many other opportunities left for an introvert.

Online dating, though, comes with plenty of obstacles, such as people lying and posting faked pictures. It is difficult enough to communicate in a one-on-one, facing each other in reality. Talking online with people, who understand communication as an exchange of word fragments or not answering questions at all, is just frustrating. It is unbelievable, how dangerous online dating can be if you get in the wrong lane!

Nonetheless, one day I made an interesting acquaintance. A. was a decent, well-mannered and extroverted man and an IT project manager like me at the time. As soon as he had contacted me, I knew this was not going to work. *He hasn't got a clue who he is dealing with,* I thought with a sigh. People are so oblivious to the obvious when physical needs overrule the spiritual ones. Anyway, in the end we had managed to turn our encounter into friendship. This went so far that I gave advice on how he could find the right woman. Isn't that funny?

One day, we met for an amicable walk in the beautiful area of *Lake Constance*. I remember it so well because it was supposed to become a real eye-opener for me. It's a great advantage if you can talk seriously to a man who isn't trying to get in your panties. You can speak quite frankly about anything. So we did.

At some point, I worked up the courage to ask him why he had shied away from a love affair with me. At first, he hemmed and hawed, but finally, he decided to spill the beans. "*You are a power-woman*," A. said hesitantly. He must have thought that his vague statement explained everything. Blankly, I stared at him: "*And, - what is that supposed to mean?*" Searching for words, he started fidgeting. After stammering a few half-baked sentences, I got the gist of the matter. A. seemed to be intimidated by my skills and hobbies. He was not used to women communicating honestly without pretence, nor trying to avoid the subject.

That shut me up. For a moment, there was silence. I could not believe it. There I was, having honed my skills and worked on forming my character over the years to become a better person. Apparently, it was all for nothing, because men feared to face the challenge and to lose face, should they not be able to live up to it. Great! Why hadn't anyone told me earlier? Ok, I would have done it anyway. It would not have changed anything, but honestly! However, after I had regained my countenance, I was grateful to have been told the truth. It helped me immensely to understand the reactions of men in my past. Besides, it is rare to gain insight into the brain of a man.

Not knowing that I am an introvert, I always struggled with connections to extroverts. The kind of my upbringing did not allow me to end a relationship just on the ground of uneasiness. Once, I had been very ill, and after realigning my life rigorously, everything changed. As if a veil had been lifted from my eyes, I could see clearly that the time of compromises was over. As hard and painful as it was, - I cut off any kind of relationship that was not good for me, including the ones to my two older siblings – good riddance!

There comes a moment when one needs to realise that it is not wise to comply with every rule you have been taught. It is essential to find out who you are and what rules are right for you. This is no easy task because it calls into question everything that we have considered being the law. But if we manage, life gets easier afterwards.

I don't imply that relationships between introverts and extroverts would not work in general. It just does not work for me, with one exception, and that is my Twin Soul OSIRIS.

## Twin Souls

Extroverts can escape solitude in going out, which gives them an advantage wherever they are, even in the office. The same applies to private relationships. Introverts are deprived of their solitude in business matters if they are not freelancers. As it turned out, absolute solitude in my private life is only possible if I live as a single person. Everything was straightforward until I met my Twin Soul in a castle abroad. Speaking of light and darkness!

It was August 2015. My daughter lived her own life, and meanwhile, as a single, I had learned to enjoy mine. That's when I met my *Twin Soul* on the *'Isle of Dreams'*. I was there on holiday with my friend H., who occasionally I am travelling the world with and who is one of the most introverted persons I ever became acquainted with. Before the journey, I had indulged in my ritual of Tarot Card reading, choosing the Oracle game. There were the King of Swords, Six of Swords and the Emperor. A significant journey had been forecast as well as travelling across the water, and a time of transition. The cards advised me not to shy away from the unknown and that it is time to explore new ways to find love. Very telling, or rather foretelling.

As stories go, my friend H. and I had not planned to visit that particular castle at all. We were on our way to the next hotel when I saw a sign. I asked my companion spontaneously if there was time for visiting the famous neo-classical architectural jewel. There was, and so we turned left to drive along a grand avenue of oaks near a still loch. There was an hour left before the next tour began, so we divided. My friend H., having a sweet tooth, went to try the famous chocolate cake in the café. As for me, I was more interested in visiting the second-hand bookshop under the stables' archway.

Somehow, I had hoped to find a book about myths and legends. Entering the shop, at first I did not see the man who was selling the books. Strolling along the bookshelves, I let my eyes roam over the variety of literature. Out of the blue, a voice behind me asked if I needed help. I did indeed, and an animated conversion about books took its course. We did not find what I was looking for, but then a poem book with a picture of the '*Lady of Sha-lott*' on the front cover caught my eye.

"*Do you like poems?*" the elderly man asked. "*Indeed, I do.*", I replied. Suddenly, he stood in front of me and recited the complete ballad '*The Lady of Shalott*' by *Alfred Lord Tennyson*. It happened in such a heart-breaking manner that it brought tears to my eyes. He must be a '*gentleman of the old school*', I mused. There was an instant, unusual spiritual connection between us.

Afterwards, I took a photo of him and bought the mentioned book as well as '*The collected Poems*' by *Alfred Lord Tennyson*. Since the man asked me to send him the photos, we exchanged our email addresses. Before I left the castle, I went back to the bookshop to say Goodbye again. When I found the room empty, a strange sadness enwrapped my heart.

To make a long story short, this man I met in the bookshop turned out to be my *Twin Soul* or *Twin Flame*, for that matter. He is 22 years older and proved to be an intriguing mix of introvert and extrovert. Already retired, he helped in the bookshop once a week. He wrote poetry and prose most days. An exciting exchange of letters and emails began and has not stopped since.

After two years and episodes of travelling back and forth, we tried to live together in my home. For my Twin Soul, it was Heaven. He liked this way of living very much: going out to make new acquaintances or having the spacious flat at his disposal all day while I was off to work. Unlike me, my Twin Flame loves to meet and talk with people, revelling in their attention. He is quick to adapt to nearly every situation and person. As much as he enjoys hours of complete solitude, he also needs the company of others.

For me, living together was not just a challenge but an acid test. The problems started as soon as I came home. I crave a few hours of solitude every day, but I did not get them anymore. Bravely, I faced the music and tried to ignore my own needs as I always had done in the past. I wanted him to be happy, but made myself unhappy at the same time. It is hard to explain, but I experience it as a mental and physical intrusion when someone walks through my extended aura.

As for planning things, I was not very amused when my friend told me regularly that for this evening or tomorrow, he had been invited to a party. He had known this for weeks, but just did not bother telling me. How is one supposed to plan things, if the other one does not communicate properly?

Many other things bothered me, possibly due to my partly autistic nature. After two years, it became clear that it doesn't work for the two of us living together, or well, not for me. Fortunately, he understood my difficulties. Now, we live apart again. My Twin Soul went back to the country he was born in, and I stayed in my home country. Nonetheless, our love and understanding is stronger than ever, which is manifested and illustrated in our book series "*Twin Flame Poetry-Treasury*". We are like two sides of a coin, different, but inseparable. I will always be grateful for him giving me back my solitude, where I can thrive and grow further. As we can confirm, there is truth in the saying "*Absence makes the heart grow fonder*" indeed.

Living separately also has other advantages. Poems come easier because there is space between us. Also, email-communication has started again. When we lived together, I missed this part of our connection very much.

On the other hand, misunderstandings arise more quickly in e-mails that can be cleared up faster in one-on-one talks.

By the way, isn't it a coincidence that about 10 years ago, my Twin Soul met *Jonathan Cheek* at a seminar? Its purpose was to talk about the basics of psychology and how to apply aspects of it in everyday-living. He led a group of twelve people who learned how the mind works as well as how culture and the environment interact with the individual. Also, Cheek taught ways to better understand ourselves and others. Fostering positive interaction was another topic. The seminar was an unforgettable experience.

## Sit with me in Silence

*Sit with me in silence: hold my hand*
*With the hand of your mind*
*I'll be your shadow; you'll be mine*

*We'll rest in two dimensions*
*Watch ourselves in 3D*
*Safe in the warmth*
*Of our common intentions*
*A womb, a room for you and me*

*Let's communicate like mountains*
*Be like solid, quiet giants*
*Sit with me in silence*

*A river dug into purest stone*
*After uncountable years reflecting*
*Sunlight, moonlight, stars*
*And blue skies not rejecting*
*Dark clouds too, in divine alliance*

*And there, within its deepest deep*
*Two single, uncut diamonds*
*Until we're ground to grains of sand*
*Sit with me in silence*

OSIRIS (2015)

# Introversion and Autism

According to Wikipedia, *"Autism is a developmental disorder of variable severity that is characterized by difficulty in social interaction and communication and by restricted or repetitive patterns of thought and behaviour."*

(Wikipedia. "n.d.". Autism. Retrieved from https://en.wikipedia.org/wiki/Autism)

That sounds quite serious, but also a bit too limited, if you ask me. Lots of signs of autism have been defined that may indicate a person has autism. The following signs apply to me, I think:

- *"Avoiding eye contact*
- *Reliance on rules and routines*
- *Being upset by relatively minor changes*
- *Unexpected reactions to sounds, tastes, sights, touch and smells*
- *Be under- or over-sensitive to loud noises, strong smells or tastes*
- *Have a good memory and recall of facts*
- *Spending time alone to escape social interaction*

- *Lacking interest in playing social games or being around others*
- *Using of formal language rather than the slang of their peers*
- *Developing strong preferences for certain foods, clothes or objects"*

(Ada's Medical Knowledge Team. "n.d.". Signs of Autism. Retrieved from https://ada.com/ signs-of-autism/)

However, I do make eye contact with people I like and feel safe with. *Avoiding eye contact* with strangers or people I don't like is one of my consciously chosen methods to keep them from approaching me. Eyes can be weapons, and for some, they are what the nectar is for the bees, which I find quite dangerous, especially for me.

*Relying or insisting on rules and routines* is indeed something that comforts me immensely. It saves a lot of time if I know what to expect and where to find things. So, it is just natural that I get upset at even relatively minor changes to routines. It does not mean a lack of flexibility, though. I am talking about routines and rules of my private life only. You could say that I am a fierce defender of my privacy.

In my job, the first rule is to be flexible, and I have no problem doing justice to this.

Aesthetic and the simplicity of *designs* and *patterns* are very important to me too. A composition must not just please the eye, but the spirit as well. I like to position my things in an orderly, precise and harmonious way. Funny enough, some people think that I would like only rectangular forms. They are far off the mark. In fact, I have a penchant for round, rolling, octagonal and rhombic shapes. When I put things in a particular order or angle, I do it subconsciously and get deeply upset, if someone changes it.

Once, a friend gave me a set of earrings and necklace as a birthday present. The colour was brilliant, but the shape of the earrings was not. They were rectangular and in such a position that I could not bear to wear them. Thus, I decided to dismantle and to fix them in a different angle. Since then, they are my favourites.

*"Using of formal language rather than the slang of their peers"* is another revealing aspect. I remember that someone had commented on that point when my daughter was about 16 months old. During a walk in a park, she caught sight

of a dog and had explained proudly: *"Mama, there is a dog."* A by-standing mother wondered why my daughter had not used baby-talk and the word *'bow-wow'*. Furthermore, she was astonished that my daughter had formed a full sentence, albeit a simple one. Well, my daughter never used baby-talk. She only pronounced words she could speak correctly. Children repeat what they hear and since I spoke clearly and in whole sentences, - why shouldn't she?

At times, I get the impression that some of the characteristics of introversion blend seamlessly into those of autism. Last year, I made an autism test on the internet and came up with more than half of the results being positive. Of course, that doesn't mean I'm a full-blown autistic. But at least a certain tendency towards autism is recognisable. Afterwards, I thought to myself: *Since autism is called a disorder, introversion might be regarded as one too. What is the order then? Extroversion? I hope not...*

# Misconceptions

M isconceptions are part of the package, I think. As an innate hermit, I know what I am talking about. Some people think of us introverts as *rude*. To protect ourselves and our privacy, we did not need to appear *rude* if extroverts would begin respecting our boundaries. When somebody oversteps our borderlines, - that is what I'd call rude. With a little more mutual understanding, we could avoid misconceptions altogether.

It is another common misconception that people take us for *reserved natures* because we keep to ourselves. They even think we hate others. Ok, that might be partly true. But in general, we just want to be left alone and like to decide, if, and when we meet someone. We don't like to be boxed into situations, where we need to talk ourselves out in a possibly rude manner.

Solitude is important for our sanity and well-being. Even though we love others, there are times when the need arises to get away from them. No offence intended. Introverts understand that need, whereas extroverts might feel rejected.

We have seen that in my family, the introverted nature has many different facets, even in one person. The best thing is to take people as they are, without judging or complaining. Extroverts and introverts alike know very well how to enjoy themselves. It is just different.

As my parents were, I am a born *leader* and worked as such successfully for many years. However, I don't enjoy being a manager, but I prefer to sit quietly in a single office, working in solitude. The assertion that introverted people are *poor leaders* is simply not true. It's the opposite, and we don't tend to take all the credit for group successes either. Neither do we step into the spotlight all the time. What is wrong with that? The downside might be that we are less noticeable, but that's not the point, is it? Usually, we don't depend on external motivation. Often, we are pleased enough with the inner satisfaction of having done something well.

On another website, I came across a quotation from Susan Cain: *"It makes sense that so many introverts hide even from themselves. We live with a value system that I call the Extrovert Ideal — the omnipresent belief that the ideal self is gregarious, alpha, and comfortable in the spotlight."*

(Susan Cain. "n.d.". Quiet Quotes. Retrieved from https://www.goodreads.com/ quotes/6606660-it-makes-sense-that-so-many-introverts-hide-even-from)

The latter statement we can agree on. The first point, though, does not make sense to me. Why would introverted persons hide from themselves? Is this even possible? People can hide from others, but not from themselves. This would require two different kinds of consciousness in one person. I have never met such people. One simply cannot outrun oneself, not even in closing off messages consciousness or sub-consciousness deliver. Let's just say that we like to keep a low profile.

As I have observed, we introverts create our own beautiful inner world where we live and not just survive. This is necessary to replenish our depleted resources. In our happy places, we can be who we are. If we would hide from ourselves, we had nowhere to go. Why would we do that? Our inner world is invisible to others anyway. No one can disturb or harm us there. That's our only save haven we return to every day.

If, and when we are free to live up to our true nature, then we introverts are at ease. Destined to achieve great things, we go forwards bravely. To fight and to win, we fathom and embrace the mysteries of our aptitudes at some point. Only then, we can project the beauty of our inner world into outer realms. Like the beacon of a lighthouse, we become saviours of others, calming the troubled waters in this vast ocean of life.

During a conversation about introversion with a friend, the question arose whether only introverts have a quiet temperament. Well, I don't know if that applies to every type of introvert or if it excludes extroverts. A quiet temperament is probably not something that only introverts can lay claim to. I have met many extroverts who are quiet. Or take me, for example: many people would describe me as the opposite. I assume that the real, hidden power lies in the sum of our advantages as introverts.

Some people seem to think we introverts would not make an impression. Then, others claim we make good role models. As for the latter, I agree. My Scottish friend I., who is 15 years older than me, told me once that she would see me as a role model for herself. I was astonished about that because until then, I had assumed that role models are supposed to be older. Besides, I was not aware that I could serve as an example for other people. Now I know better. Isn't it beautiful, how much friends can learn from each other, no matter the age?

Thinking back, I just realized that all my life, my mother was a role model for me. Most of all, I admired her strength, restraint, wisdom and her ability to see the best in everyone and everything. My mother is the incarnation of love, light and magic. The older I became, the more I wanted to be like her and to deserve her respect. But I know that this will never happen, for I need to be myself…

# Conclusion

As *Jenn Granneman, Susan Cain* and many other introverts, I am on a mission. Not that I would want to open another blog on the internet. This is not my way. I am content to share my knowledge in private conversations and in writing this book. To be frank, I was never drawn to internet communities, but I know some people need such places. They provide them with perfect opportunities to communicate without being seen.

Much has been written about introverts and extroverts, but I am still cautious about the accuracy of some definitions. The more or less proven knowledge about introversion, I do not understand as a means to define my personality. However, I see it as a clear possibility to reflect and to understand myself and others better to improve life and well-being.

What I wonder about is why we don't learn anything in school about introversion, temperament or character-building at all. Instead, we are forced to memorize all types of spiders and other unnecessary information. Of course,

I have my suspicion and a theory about that. My guess is that nothing has changed considerably since the Roman poet *Juvenal* wrote in a satire about *"Panem et Circenses"*. He complained that ordinary people wanted nothing more than bread and entertainment. It might not be far-fetched that even nowadays, many people wish exactly for that. Everything else is hard work, especially thinking about oneself or even worse, changing oneself.

Obviously, teaching children about personalities and virtues they are born with and how to deal with them is not in the interest of state or industry. It makes it so much easier to suppress introverts if they think that something is wrong with them. The extroverts are even better to deal with because they tend to launch into everything that keeps them from their own company. Talking about the colourful world of multi-media...

It cannot be a coincidence that the multimedia industry has been growing into a maze of nearly unmanageable crossroads and choices. TVs have become as big as the walls they are attached to. The variety of games, music and public events seems to have no limits either. This is not just about money for the movers and shakers. People are lured to distract themselves with leisure activities. That leaves them neither the time nor inclination to connect with their inner worlds, much less to think about improving themselves.

Another point is that a large measure of the high potential we introverts are born with is systematically wasted. This shows especially in the open-space offices, - made for extroverts only. It continues when it comes to job applications, where extroverts have a much better chance to succeed because they know how to sell a fridge to the Inuit.

While writing the book, I came to know my loved ones and myself in a new and different way. In the beginning, I took those definitions about the four types of introverts as rules set in stone. Yet, during the process of writing, fascinating insights surfaced. At some point, I began to understand that definitions don't have to be fixed. On the contrary, they need to be flexible, especially when it comes to human nature.

Furthermore, I realised that writing a book is not just about relating a hero's journey, but also means going on a hero's journey myself. Isn't that marvellous? If you come out of the woods alive, you are a changed person indeed. Of course, that is not the end of it, for it is just the beginning of another tantalising journey.

Everyone is unique, that is not every rule applies to anyone, especially since we change considerably throughout the years. There are abilities and conditions we bring into our lives, and then there are developed ones. I am a person who needs rules for stability reasons, and this is not going to change. But I have discovered the necessity to adjust the rules to the states of my spiritual development. Although self-enquiry can be a real joy, - pain and pleasure are never far apart. So, whatever writers or other people tell you about introversion, it is not the law. I prefer to interpret their opinions as possibilities I have yet to check. I rather see them as an encouragement to explore open-minded the truth that works for my unique essence. This sounds easy, but it is hard work, especially for a person who deep down does not like changes.

Every introvert needs to develop their own strategy to deal with introversion. That also means to let go of negative emotions towards extroverts. There are no universal rules except one, I think. If it feels good, makes you happy and you can be yourself, then you are on the right track. I wish, I had known of my mother's, my daughter's and my introversion earlier. Then, our lives might have been different, as had been many a choice. Yet, I go with the saying "*Better late than never.*" Even though I self-discovered being an introvert quite late at the age of 45, I still call it '*Snatching victory from the jaws of defeat!*' To realise that introversion is not a flaw but a virtue, was life-changing for me.

My hope is that with every written article and book, the tide will turn a little bit more. I encourage every introvert to stay true to thyself and to find the spiritedness to do what feels right, - no matter what other people say or do. It is the only way to realize our full potential and to reach higher levels of consciousness.

Say NO without feeling guilty, and remember that you don't need to explain why you do this and leave that. This is *your* life, and *you* should be the only one to determine its course.

Never forget that every aspect of your unique introverted nature is a treasure. Live up to your own expectations and not to those of others. You are whole and you are perfect!

Don't let others make your decisions. Be brave and change your life radically, if necessary. It does not matter *how many* people agree with you, but *who* does, and this one person is you. To become and be who you are is not just a privilege, but an obligation. It is the very goal of your life to know thyself and to live up to it. The journey is worth its while.

Rumi was of the opinion: *"You are not a drop in the ocean. You are the entire ocean in a drop."* Yes, together we can rock the waves. Let's join forces and do it!

Sabine Sparakowski

## Five Dimensions

*In the first dimension*
*Of human beings*
*Our bodies lived*
*Through vital energy*
*Constant reminders of*
*Magnetism and gravity*

*Shaped Flowers of life*
*The next one lingers:*
*Source of immortal seeds*
*Fruits and emotions*
*Subtle levels bear feelings*
*And karmic circles alike*

*Conjoined with the third*
*In limited space are*
*Fire and Air, water and ether*
*In daring spheres of the will*
*The reason is growing*
*As energy is flowing*

*Fourth dimension of contrasts*
*Bold darkness and bright light*
*Born from brilliant, infinite vastness*
*Inhaling is silver, exhaling is gold*
*Cosmic reflections of vitality:*
*A perfect matrix of 4 D projection*

*Turning into dimension five*
*Structure becomes vital*
*Colours in divine order*
*Cast fragile bonds*
*Between earth and spirit*
*Woven in perfect harmony*

ISIS (2016)

# Acknowledgements

Thank you, *Jenn Granneman*, for your great articles about *The Secret Lives of Introverts*. I thoroughly enjoyed studying them. It gave me plenty of input for reflection on introversion within my family. Also, it confirmed that it is never too late to make positive changes in one's life or to find one's calling.

Endless gratitude is extended to my wonderful *parents*, for all the stories we have made together, and the experiences of our past time. I am grateful for your love, support, understanding, and your unfailing trust in me. You encouraged me to read, to write, and to question everything. You taught me to fight, to never give up and to stay true to myself.

*"Forget safety. Live where you fear to live. Destroy your reputation. Be notorious."*

Rumi

Many thanks to my beloved *daughter* I share so many beautiful memories with. Your support in proofreading was very welcome. You helped me in times when I was down and thought that my life was over. Every time, when I look at your face, I know that I did at least one thing right! As my mother, you are like the never wavering light of a candle in the darkness.

*"It is your light that lights the worlds."*

Rumi

Thank you very much, all my German *friends*, who shared the results of their intro-version-check with me, although it was in English. Sorry about that! You have accompanied me faithfully for so many years, and I hope there are more to come.

*"Friend, our closeness is this: anywhere you put your foot, feel me in the firmness under you."*

Rumi

Now, my *Twin Soul*, thank you for believing in me, loving me, and giving me the much-craved solitude to breathe, to blossom, and to write this book. Also, I am grateful for your help with proofreading.

*"Goodbyes are only for those who love with their eyes. Because for those who love with heart and soul there is no such thing as separation."*

Rumi

I'm eternally grateful to the great *team of Moniack Mhor*, Scotland's Creative Writing Centre amid the picturesque Scottish Highlands. With heart and soul, you organized the courses and made me feel at home every time I was there. It is the perfect place to write or meditate in solitude, especially in the atmospheric Hobbit-House *"below the starry clusters bright"*, as *Alfred Lord Tennyson* put it in his ballad *'The Lady of Shalott'* so well.

*"Start a huge, foolish project, like Noah…*
*It makes absolutely no difference what people think of you."*

Rumi

Special thanks to my tutors *Ann & Peter Sansom* of the Poetry Course in 2017 and to *Joan Lennon* and *Paul Magrs* who led the Young Adult Fantasy Course in 2018 at Moniack

Mhor. *Joan,* you particularly encouraged me to continue writing and allayed my doubts. *"I know that one day you will write that book,"* you said. Every time I start to falter, your words come back and keep me going.

*"You will never do anything in this world without courage. It is the greatest quality in the mind next to honour."*

Aristotle

FSC
www.fsc.org

MIX

Papier | Fördert
gute Waldnutzung

FSC® C083411

Zeitfracht Medien GmbH
Ferdinand-Jühlke-Straße 7
99095 Erfurt, Deutschland
produktsicherheit@kolibri360.de